About this Learning Guide

Shmoop Will Make You a Better Lover*
*of Literature, History, Poetry, Life...

Our lively learning guides are written by experts and educators who want to show your brain a good time. Shmoop writers come primarily from Ph.D. programs at top universities, including Stanford, Harvard, and UC Berkeley.

Want more Shmoop? We cover literature, poetry, bestsellers, music, US history, civics, biographies (and the list keeps growing). Drop by our website to see the latest.

www.shmoop.com

Table of Contents

shmoop

Introduction

In a Nutshell

Kurt Vonnegut is probably most associated with the 1960s and its crazy experimental fiction. But before he became popular with Bohemians and hippies, Vonnegut was a soldier, fighting in World War II as an American advance infantry scout in the 106th Division. His first deployment in Europe was to fight back the last major German offensive of the war, the Battle of the Bulge. Vonnegut was captured by the Germans and brought to Dresden, where he was kept in relatively decent conditions in one of the most beautiful cities in Europe.

If you think this is all building up to something awful, you're right. On February 13, 1945, while Vonnegut was in Dresden as an American POW (prisoner of war), Allied bombers dropped a huge wave of "incendiary devices" on the city – bombs made of super explosive materials like phosphorus and jellied petroleum (a.k.a. napalm for you Vietnam War buffs out there). Dresden went up in flames and pretty much the entire city was destroyed. This single firebombing had a death toll, the novel tells us, of 135,000 people, though there is some debate about actual numbers. (Read more about Dresden here.)

Even now, the jury is out about whether the Dresden firebombing, with its high number of civilian deaths, was militarily necessary. Whatever historians may think about the deaths at Dresden, Vonnegut certainly felt that he had witnessed "the largest single massacre in military history," worse even than the Hiroshima and Nagasaki atom bombings (source: Klinkowitz, Jerome. *Slaughterhouse-Five: Reforming the Novel and the World*. Boston: Twayne Publishers, 1990. Pg. 4).

It took a while before Vonnegut could really write about his experiences during the Dresden firebombing, and not just because it was so personally painful. The firebombing was classified top-secret for years. Vonnegut explicitly points out the troubles he had getting information on the bombing from the Air Force in Chapter 1, Section 7.

Slaughterhouse-Five finally came out in 1969, 25 years after the Dresden firebombing, but only one year after the hugely unpopular Vietnam War Tet Offensive, just as the anti-war movement really started to intensify in the U.S. In the middle of growing demands to end the war in Vietnam, *Slaughterhouse-Five* seemed to express the emerging popular horror at the idea of war. With its hugely successful publication, Vonnegut cemented his reputation as *the* spokesman for America's 1960s and 1970s counterculture.

Why Should I Care?

A common topic of discussion over here on the Shmoop couch after we have just finished watching an episode of _America's Next Top Model_ or _Project Runway_ is that life is not fair. In fact, you may have noticed that life is often actively cruel. Our favorite models get dinged early, talented singers come in second on _American Idol_...the injustice of it all! We have all occasionally found existence meaningless or hard to get through, and we find various ways (like, say, reality TV or Sherlock Holmes novels) to cope.

Billy Pilgrim, the main character of *Slaughterhouse-Five*, has *way* more proof than we do of how crummy life can be. He is, after all, a prisoner of war and witness to one of the most horrible massacres in history. Who can blame Billy for escaping into crappy science fiction whenever life gets a bit much? In fact, his pain is so deep and goes so far beyond our day-to-day relationship and family troubles that he really starts to lose himself, literally, in fiction.

Slaughterhouse-Five is a book about war, but even more than that, it's about what comes *after* war, when someone who has lived through it has to rebuild his sense of self. Billy's trips to the alien planet Tralfamadore and his fanboy relationship with sci-fi author Kilgore Trout are way more extreme than our weekly *Top Model* catharsis. But it's a difference of degree rather than kind. We all sometimes need a refuge from our lives. And Billy's reality is so much worse than ours that we can totally see why he decides to go on a permanent mental vacation.

Book Summary

It's hard to summarize the plot of *Slaughterhouse-Five* because everything is going on at the same time. Since the main character, Billy Pilgrim, travels through time, we jump from 1944 to 1967 to Billy's childhood and back again. We're going to try to keep this summary at least somewhat chronological, but bear in mind that the only way you'll be able to get a sense of the crazy detours and switchbacks that characterize the novel is by reading it. (And, of course, you can also consult our "Detailed Summary" if you get confused along the way.)

Slaughterhouse-Five starts with the narrator. He never officially announces, "Hello, I am Kurt Vonnegut," but he is clearly speaking as Vonnegut. He talks about the difficulty he has trying to find ways to write about his experiences in Dresden during World War II, and he makes references both to teaching at the University of Iowa's famous writing program *and* studying anthropology at the University of Chicago – both of which Kurt Vonnegut did in real life. The narrator introduces us to the two people to whom the book is dedicated: Mary O'Hare and

Vonnegut talks about difficulties to write about war experiences

Gerhard Müller. For more on these two and their significance, check our "Characters" section.

After this autobiographical intro, we get to the book itself, which stars a fairly pathetic young man named Billy Pilgrim. Billy is in optometry school (optometrists are the guys who fit you with glasses if you have eye problems) in upstate New York in 1944 when he gets drafted into the army. He isn't even a fully trained soldier; his job is to be the chaplain's assistant, leading his regiment in hymns to keep their spirits up. Nevertheless, despite his complete lack of suitability for war, Billy is deployed to Luxembourg in December 1944 to fight the Germans in the Battle of the Bulge.

Once Billy gets to the battlefield, he becomes utterly confused; he isn't even carrying a gun. He is left walking through enemy territory like a lost lamb until he gets picked up by another American recruit, a crazy bully with a love of torture implements named Roland Weary. Weary becomes so angry at Billy's lack of interest in saving his own life that he threatens to shoot him. Just as Weary is aiming at Billy, a group of German soldiers take both men prisoner. Weary winds up dying on the trek from Luxembourg to a prisoner of war (POW) camp in Germany, blaming Billy for his capture all the while.

Billy arrives by train at a prison compound in the middle of a German death camp for Russian soldiers. The compound houses mainly British troops, who have all been prisoners since near the beginning of the war. These soldiers have been eating well and exercising for most of the war, so they're in great spirits – and they're pretty disgusted by the state of the American recruits, especially weak, clownish Billy Pilgrim. It's in the British compound that Billy meets Edgar Derby, a high school teacher who will be shot at the end of the war for looting, and Paul Lazzaro, a total psycho who promises to send an assassin to kill Billy after the war for letting Roland Weary die.

Billy and Edgar Derby are both sent to a POW center in Dresden, Germany, to wait out the war. This POW camp is located in an abandoned slaughterhouse (see "What's Up With the Title?" for why this matters). Soon after they arrive in Dresden (on February 13, 1945), American bomber units attack the city, setting fires that end up consuming pretty much all of Dresden. Thousands of people die. (For more on the Dresden firebombing, check out "In a Nutshell.") Billy and a small group of his POW comrades have to climb through the ruins of buildings and bodies to find water and shelter. It's Billy's job, as a prisoner of war, to help dig bodies out of the rubble of the city.

When Billy is finally freed, following the German surrender in May, 1945, he goes back to upstate New York and starts up optometry school again. He gets engaged to Valencia, the daughter of the school's owner. Then, suddenly, he has a nervous breakdown and checks himself into a veteran's hospital to recover. Supposedly, he does get better – but after that, Billy will find himself suddenly crying, silently and without apparent reason.

Flash forward about two decades and Billy has two children: a daughter, Barbara, and a son,

Robert. Robert was kind of a wild kid as a teenager, but now he is a Marine fighting in Vietnam. Barbara – well, we'll get to her in a minute. Billy and Valencia have been (mostly) happily married for twenty years when everything goes wrong. Billy gets into an airplane with his father-in-law, Lionel. The plane crashes into the side of a mountain in Vermont and everyone except Billy is killed. Billy suffers an intense skull fracture. While Billy recovers in the hospital, Valencia dies of carbon monoxide poisoning in her car.

At the hospital, Billy rooms with an extremely energetic 70-year-old named Bertram Copeland Rumfoord, who is recuperating from a broken leg he got on a ski trip with his 23-year-old wife. Rumfoord is a historian who wants to write a book about the Air Force. He wants to include a blurb about Dresden, but he is frustrated because a lot of information about the raid is still classified.

Rumfoord does not see why the Air Force won't tell the world about such a *fantastic, successful* raid. He thinks it's because they are worried about the opinions of a bunch of bleeding hearts who might disapprove of the burning deaths of 135,000 non-combatants. Billy tells Rumfoord that he was at Dresden during the firebombing. Rumfoord wants to convince Billy that the raid was absolutely necessary, no matter how terrible it was to experience on the ground.

As Billy regains his ability to move around, he suddenly appears on a talk-radio show in New York talking about his experiences *not* as a POW – but as an alien abductee. He writes to the local paper in his hometown to tell the world about the people of the planet of Tralfamadore. (We actually hear about Tralfamadore in the second chapter of the book, but chronologically, this takes place quite late in Billy's life.) Billy's aliens are green and shaped like toilet plungers. Billy explains that they took him and a young actress named Montana Wildhack to be part of a zoo exhibition the year before. The Tralfamadorians, Billy tells the public, have a lot to teach us about time.

The Tralfamadorians see everything differently because their vision works in four dimensions. Thanks to this, they know that every moment in time is separate, eternal, and happening at the same time as every other moment. So when you see someone die, they may not be doing so well in that particular moment, but in all of the moments before then, they're still great. Death itself is an illusion, as is free will. Each point in time has always and will always be exactly the same. There is nothing we can do to change it, which, Billy thinks, should be a comfort to all of us.

Barbara, Billy's daughter, is incredibly embarrassed that he has announced all this in the newspaper, and insists on taking control of his life because he cannot care for himself anymore. It's probably not helping Billy's case for his own sanity that, during all of his arguments with Barbara and his experiences in the hospital, he keeps skipping in and out of time. His visits to Tralfamadore, his wartime captivity, and his life with his family all seem to be happening simultaneously.

See, Billy is really receptive to the Tralfamadorian way of looking at things, because he has been disconnected from time since 1944. He has seen his own birth and death many, many times, so he is uniquely qualified to believe that each independent moment is its own complete world. After all, this is both how Billy experiences time and how the novel is told – scene by scene in tiny chunks of narrative that only make sense when you look at them all at once.

The novel ends with Billy digging through the rubble of Dresden to find bodies for cremation. After finishing his job, he and his POW pals are sent to a stable to wait out the rest of the war. When the war in Europe ends, the stable door opens. Outside, all is silence except for the sounds of the birds singing, "*Poo-tee-weet*?"

Chapter 1, Section 1

- According to the narrator, "All this happened, more or less."
- Which parts really happened? The narrator goes back to Dresden, Germany, with an old war buddy, Bernard V. O'Hare. He's been in World War II, where he witnessed the Dresden firestorm (see "In a Nutshell" for more on this).
- The narrator and O'Hare ride in a taxi with a German cab driver named Gerhard Müller. Müller takes them to the slaughterhouse where they were kept as prisoners of war.
- Müller sends O'Hare a postcard wishing him, his family, and his friend (our narrator) a Merry Christmas and a happy New Year. He hopes they'll all meet again, "if the accident will" (1.1.5) – or, in other words, by chance.

Chapter 1, Section 2

- The narrator returns from his first stay in Germany as a prisoner of war 23 years before the beginning of the novel.
- He's having a lot of trouble finding words, even now.
- Look, dirty limericks, right there in the fourth paragraph! This book is a *trip*.
- Once, the narrator was talking to filmmaker Harrison Starr; he tells the guy that yes, he's writing an anti-war book.
- Starr replies that he may as well write an anti-*glacier* book. After all, you've got about as much chance of stopping a war as you do of stopping a glacier.
- And even if you could stop war, there would still be death.

Chapter 1, Section 3

- When the narrator was a bit younger, he got drunk one night and called up his old buddy,

Bernard V. O'Hare, to ask if he could visit.
- This Bernard V. O'Hare and the narrator were captured together during the war.
- O'Hare says sure, the narrator can visit – but he doesn't remember much about the whole war thing.
- The narrator tells O'Hare what the climax of the book should be: the execution of Edgar Derby. After all the people are killed in Dresden, after the war ends, the climax of the book should be the shooting of an American soldier by firing squad for stealing a teapot from the ruins of the city. Oh the irony, says the narrator.
- O'Hare seems uncomfortable.

Chapter 1, Section 4

- The narrator tells us that he's outlined this book on Dresden a million times.
- The prettiest outline ever is the one he makes on the back of a piece of wallpaper with his kid's crayons. All the characters get different colors (red, blue, yellow); the yellow line stops when his character dies. The firestorm itself is a bar of orange across the page; all the colors of the people who survive continue on the other side.
- Where all the lines stop is at a field where thousands of prisoners of war are about to be released.
- There's an exchange going on: non-Soviet troops (Americans, Western Europeans, Canadians, South Africans, etc.) are being traded for Soviet troops (Russians, Poles, Yugoslavians).
- Remember, 1945, when World War II ends, is when the Cold War between the Soviets, the U.S., and Western Europe really starts up. After Germany's surrender, East Germany (of which Dresden is part) becomes part of the Soviet bloc. So both the capitalist and communist countries want to make sure that none of their troops end up on the wrong side of the Iron Curtain.
- The narrator keeps a souvenir: a Luftwaffe (German air force) saber.
- A bunch of other guys keep things too, that they've gotten out of the burned rubble of Dresden.
- All the Allied prisoners of war wind up in a rest camp in France.
- The narrator heads home, gets married, and has kids.
- Now his kids are grown, and he's just an old guy.
- He likes to make phone calls late at night to people he used to know a long time ago – in this case, girlfriends.
- He lets his dog in or out. He tells the dog, Sandy, that he likes him.
- He'll turn on talk radio coming out of Boston and New York.
- Occasionally he thinks about the time he spent after the war studying anthropology at the University of Chicago. There, he learned that there is absolutely no difference between people.
- He remembers that, before his dad died, he pointed out that none of the narrator's books

have villains. The narrator told his father that that's something he learned in college, after the war.

Chapter 1, Section 5

- During college, the narrator works for the Chicago City News Bureau.
- The narrator tells us about the first story he ever reported, about a poor guy just back from the war working as an elevator operator.
- He's supposed to bring the elevator down to the basement, but his wedding ring gets caught in the metal ornaments surrounding the elevator, and the elevator squashes his body.
- So the narrator calls in this story to this lady writer for her to type up. And she asks him: how did the poor shmo's wife respond? The wife doesn't know yet, says our narrator.
- The writer tells the narrator to call the wife posing as a member of the police department so he can get the wife's initial reaction to her husband's death.
- Our narrator does call the wife. And she responds with "about what you would expect her to say" (1.5.10).
- When he calls back with the wife's reaction, the woman writer asks what the guy's body looked like after being squashed – just because she wants to know.
- The narrator tells her. (We find out that her name is Nancy.) It doesn't bother him, he says, because he's seen lots worse in the war.

Chapter 1, Section 6

- The narrator changes subjects: even though he's writing a book on Dresden, it's not a well-known air raid in the States. Lots of Americans don't know that more people died there than in the bombing of Hiroshima.
- He meets a guy at a University of Chicago cocktail party who tells him about concentration camps where Germans made soap and candles out of the rendered fat of Jewish bodies.
- The narrator can only say, "I know, I know. *I know*" (1.64).

Chapter 1, Section 7

- The narrator then goes on to what he calls the scrawny years, when he and his wife had lost all of their baby fat.
- He's a P.R. guy for General Electric in Schenectady, New York.

- All the nicest people he meets in Schenectady, the people who really hate war, are people who'd fought the hardest during the war.
- The narrator writes to the Air Force about the Dresden air raid, asking who ordered it, how many planes were involved, and what their objectives were.
- The Air Force writes back and says that all this is still top-secret.
- Our narrator reads this letter aloud to his wife and says, "Secret? My God – from *whom*?" (1.69).

Chapter 1, Section 8

- This is a super short section, only four sentences long:

  We were United World Federalists back then. I don't know what we are now. Telephoners, I guess. We telephone a lot – or I do, anyway, late at night.

Chapter 1, Section 9

- A couple of weeks after calling O'Hare, our narrator really does go to see him. This would've been in 1964, the year of the New York World's Fair.
- He brings his daughter Nanny and her best friend with him. It's the first time the two girls have ever left Cape Cod. They've never seen a river before.
- They all arrive at O'Hare's house.

Chapter 1, Section 10

- The narrator meets O'Hare's wife, Mary, who's a very nice lady. But for all of her niceness to his kids and her ease with entertaining, there's *something* that shows that she just doesn't *like* our narrator.
- Mary brings the narrator and O'Hare into the kitchen to talk and leaves them to it, but she's obviously *furious* about something. She's banging around all over the house, walking around, opening and closing doors, even moving furniture.
- O'Hare is embarrassed at his wife's anger. But he won't say why she's so pissed.
- The narrator and O'Hare try to come up with some war stories but they can't think of anything good.
- Mary finally comes into the kitchen for a soda. At last, she confronts our narrator. She yells that they were just *babies* when they went to war, but in his book, they'll seem like men.

She thinks he's going to write some book glorifying their war experience. That book will be made into a movie starring Frank Sinatra and John Wayne, and it's going to make war seem like so much fun that they're going to have lots more.
- Finally, the narrator gets it.

Chapter 1, Section 11

- So the narrator promises Mary that, if this book ever gets finished, there will be no part for Frank Sinatra or John Wayne.
- He tells her that he'll call it the Children's Crusade (see "What's Up with the Title?" for more on this).
- Mary likes that.

Chapter 1, Section 12

- After this, the narrator and O'Hare go into the living room to look up the Children's Crusade in a book called *Extraordinary Popular Delusions and the Madness of Crowds*.
- The author of this book, Charles Mackay, thinks the whole Crusade thing was pretty dumb in the first place, what with the loss of millions of lives and lots of money just so a few knights could hang onto Palestine for a hundred years.
- The Children's Crusade was only slightly dumber than most wars: in 1213, two monks decided to raise armies of faithful kids in Germany and France to sell them as slaves in North Africa.
- About thirty thousand kids volunteered to fight the Ottoman Empire for control of Jerusalem. About half of them drowned in shipwrecks. The other half made it to North Africa, where they probably were sold into slavery.
- A few of the children went to Genoa, Italy, by accident. The people of Genoa gave them some money to go home.
- Mary O'Hare cheers for the people of Genoa.
- The narrator goes upstairs to sleep. O'Hare has left him a book, published in 1908, on the history and artistic development of the city of Dresden. (This book is called *Dresden: History, Stage, Gallery*, by Mary Endell.)
- The book reports that, in 1760, Dresden suffered from a siege by the Prussians. A lot of the city's art work and beautiful buildings were destroyed.
- There is an account of this siege by the famous German poet and writer, Johann Wolfgang van Goethe.

Chapter 1, Section 13

- After this visit, the narrator takes his daughter and her friend to the New York World's Fair.

Chapter 1, Section 14

- For a couple of years after this, our narrator teaches at the Writer's Workshop at the University of Iowa – which, by the way, is hugely famous. He teaches in the afternoon and writes his book on Dresden in the morning.
- And somewhere in there, he gets a three-book contract with a man named Seymour Lawrence.
- The first of those books? His book about Dresden. Which is this book.

Chapter 1, Section 15

- This is short and confusing because it has to be: what do you say about a massacre? The point of killing everybody is that they can't say or want anything ever again.
- All that's left after a massacre is the birds, and they just say birdie things – like *Poo-tee-weet*.

Chapter 1, Section 16

- The narrator has told his sons that they are not allowed:
- (a) to take part in massacres;
- (b) to be excited about massacres...

Chapter 1, Section 17

- ... or (c) to work for companies that make weapons.
- (d) They *should* feel contempt for people who believe we need weapons.

Chapter 1, Section 18

- Our narrator has a great time in East and West Germany with his buddy Bernard V. O'Hare. He sees a lot of great real background for future made-up stories.

Chapter 1, Section 19

- Thanks to fog the night that he and O'Hare fly back to the States, the narrator has to spend an unexpected night in a hotel in Philadelphia.

Chapter 1, Section 20

- He quotes from two books that he brought with him, with a particularly awesome reference to Louis-Ferdinand Céline, French author and vet of WWI, who screams on the page to a crowd to stop moving "so that they won't disappear anymore!" (1.20.3).

Chapter 1, Section 21

- The narrator opens his hotel's Gideon Bible and finds the story of God raining fire on Sodom and Gomorrah.
- Sure, there may have been awful people in the cities of Sodom and Gomorrah. But the person the narrator really admires is Lot's wife, who looks back at the burning cities even though she's not supposed to: a human response to such destruction.

Chapter 1, Section 22

- The narrator won't look back anymore. He's finished his war book. It begins, "Listen: Billy Pilgrim has come unstuck in time" (1.22.6), and ends, "Poo-tee-weet?" (1.22.12).

Chapter 2, Section 1

- Billy Pilgrim is unstuck in time.
- This means that he has had a chance to see both his birth and his death, and all the events in between, many, many times.
- But he has no control over his time travel – he could be anywhere in his own life at any time.

Chapter 2, Section 2

- Billy Pilgrim is born in 1922 in Ilium, New York (not a real place, by the way).
- He attends a semester of night classes at the Ilium School of Optometry (eye doctor school) before being drafted for World War II.
- During the War, his father dies in a hunting accident. Say it with me: so it goes.
- He is taken prisoner by the Germans and honorably discharged from the U.S. Army in 1945.
- Once he gets back to the States, he goes back to night school, gets engaged, and then has a mild mental breakdown.

Chapter 2, Section 3

- Billy gets electroshock therapy at a veteran's hospital and recovers from his breakdown.
- He marries his fiancée, and his father-in-law sets him up in the optometry business in Ilium.
- It turns out that Ilium has a special factory that requires all of its employees to buy a pair of safety glasses.
- This is good business for Billy, who supplies all of the foundry's frames.

Chapter 2, Section 4

- Billy gets rich in the glasses business.
- He has two kids, Barbara and Robert.
- Barbara marries another optometrist, and Billy sets up his new son-in-law in the business.
- Robert joins the army out of high school and fights in Vietnam.
- Early in 1968, Billy joins a group of optometrists in a chartered plane to a conference for optometrists in Montreal.
- The plane crashes in Vermont, killing everyone except Billy.

* While Billy is recovering from this plane crash, his wife dies accidentally of carbon-monoxide poisoning.

Chapter 2, Section 5

* Billy doesn't talk much once he gets back from the hospital after his plane crash.
* He has a scar across the top of his head.
* His daughter comes over almost every day; he also has a housekeeper.
* Then Billy goes to New York City and gets a talk radio program.
* He tells the whole world that he has been unstuck from time.
* He also tells everyone that he was abducted by aliens from the planet Tralfamadore in 1967.
* There, Tralfamadorians put Billy in a zoo, naked.
* They also made him have sex with a former movie star from earth, Montana Wildhack.

Chapter 2, Section 6

* Someone winds up telling Barbara about her dad's late-night radio broadcasts. She's really upset.
* Barbara and her husband drive down to New York to pick up Billy and take him home.
* He tells her that everything he's said about Tralfamadore is true: he was taken the night of his daughter's wedding and no one missed him because they used a time warp, so he could be away for years on Tralfamadore while only seconds have passed on Earth.
* A month after this radio incident, Billy writes a letter to the Ilium newspaper describing what the Tralfamadorians look like. They look like toilet plungers with their suction cups on the ground, pointing up at the sky. At the top of each Tralfamadorian shaft is a little hand with a green eye in its palm.
* The Tralfamadorians can see in four dimensions and feel bad that earthlings can only see in three.
* They have a lot to teach us about time.

Chapter 2, Section 7

* When Billy's first letter is published in the paper, he's working on the second one.
* The second letter tells the world that, when a person dies, he only *appears* to die. But none of those moments of his life are ever lost. Every moment is eternal.

- It's an illusion that we experience time as a progression from one moment to the next.
- When a Tralfamadorian sees a corpse, he thinks the person isn't doing so well at that particular moment. But all of the moments before then, the dead person has been just fine.
- So whenever Billy hears that someone is dead, he just says what the Tralfamadorians say: "So it goes" (2.7.3).

Chapter 2, Section 8

- Billy is typing on a massive old typewriter in the rumpus room.
- The heat has gone out in his house, but Billy hasn't noticed.
- The cockles of his heart are burning with joy: Billy is going to comfort everyone with his truth about time.
- His daughter, meanwhile, comes into the house looking for Billy.
- She panics when Billy doesn't answer, thinking that he's lying dead somewhere.
- But he's not dead; he's in the rumpus room.

Chapter 2, Section 9

- Barbara comes into the house and finds Billy in the rumpus room. She's carrying a copy of his letter to the Ilium newspaper about Tralfamadore, and she's *freaking out*.
- Barbara's 21and kind of mean because she's had too much responsibility too soon: she had to arrange her mother's funeral and she's worried that Billy has gone senile thanks to his plane crash.
- Billy is only 46 and wants to persuade Barbara that he's *not* senile, but he doesn't have time to think of his booming optometry business, because he has a higher purpose.
- That higher purpose is to show mankind the wisdom of his "little green friends" (2.9.4) on Tralfamadore.

Chapter 2, Section 10

- Barbara scolds Billy for making up stuff for the paper and humiliating her.
- She threatens to send Billy to the old age home where Billy's mother lives.
- Barbara says there's no such thing as the planet Tralfamadore.
- Billy says that Tralfamadore just can't be detected from Earth.
- Barbara, fed up, asks why he never mentioned any of this stuff before the plane crash.
- Billy answers that he never thought the time was right.

Chapter 2, Section 11

- Billy says he came unstuck in time long before he was kidnapped by the Tralfamadorians.
- During World War II, Billy is a chaplain's assistant. He's not really supposed to take part in combat missions or anything heroic; he's just there to preach faith in Jesus and play hymns on a portable organ.
- Because Billy is totally powerless to do anything important in the war, the men of his unit despise him. He's totally lonely.

Chapter 2, Section 12

- One morning, Billy is playing a hymn, "A Mighty Fortress Is Our God" (2.12.1), to the troops he's accompanying on maneuvers in the Carolinas.
- An umpire comes by Billy's detachment and tells them that someone had reported their detachment killed by a theoretical enemy. The troops have a good laugh over being thought dead as they eat their lunch.
- As Billy remembers this moment, he thinks over how much like the Tralfamadorian idea of death that had been: to eat and be dead at the same time.
- Toward the end of maneuvers, Billy has to go home because his father is shot and killed in a hunting accident.

Chapter 2, Section 13

- When Billy gets back from his emergency trip home, he's immediately sent to Europe to fight the Germans in the Battle of the Bulge.
- Billy never even gets to meet the new chaplain he's supposed to assist. He never gets a helmet or combat boots.
- He somehow manages to get lost behind enemy lines.
- He falls in with three other American soldiers (two scouts and an anti-tank gunner), none of whom have maps, food, or anything helpful.
- Billy is the most pathetic of all: he is tall and skinny and without a helmet, overcoat, weapon, or boots. Even though he's only 21, he's going bald and his beard is coming in white.

Chapter 2, Section 14

- On the third day of their wanderings behind enemy lines, someone shoots at the four guys.
- Three of them manage to duck into a ditch for cover, but Billy just stands there like an idiot. He seems to think it's the rules of fair play that he should give the marksman another chance.
- Roland Weary, the antitank gunner, yells at Billy to get out of the way, "you dumb motherfucker" (2.14.3).
- Billy is so shocked that he gets down off the road.

Chapter 2, Section 15

- Weary is working hard to save Billy, but he's got to be a jerk to do it, slapping him, kicking him, making him move.
- This is because Billy wants to quit. He wants everybody to leave him alone: "You guys go on without me" (2.15.2).

Chapter 2, Section 16

- For all his big talk, Weary is no more knowledgeable about war than Billy is.
- He has fired exactly one shot in the war. That shot leaves a black spot on the ground that shows the German tanks exactly where his gun crew is.
- The Germans fire, killing every member of the gun crew except Weary.
- So it goes.

Chapter 2, Section 17

- Weary is eighteen years old and from Pittsburgh, Pennsylvania.
- He has had an unhappy childhood: he is not popular in Pittsburgh because he's a stupid bully.
- Weary likes to attach himself to people even less popular than him, pretend to be friends for a while, and then beat the crap out of them.
- He has done this over and over again.
- Weary's father, a plumber, collects torture instruments and weapons.
- He once gave Weary's mother a working thumbscrew as a paperweight and a lamp with a model of the Iron Maiden of Nuremberg as its base. The Iron Maiden was a medieval

torture instrument, a human-sized hinged metal cabinet shaped like a woman on the outside and lined with spikes on the inside. It had a drain in the bottom for blood.

Chapter 2, Section 18

- Weary tells Billy about the Iron Maiden, dum-dums, and his father's Derringer pistol.
- (Incidentally, Weary's dum-dums aren't those tiny lollipop things; they are hollow-tipped expanding bullets.)
- Weary bets that Billy doesn't even know what a blood gutter is.
- Billy guesses that it's the drain at the bottom of the Iron Maiden.
- Weary says no, it's a groove at the side of a sword or bayonet.
- Weary tells Billy about some tortures he's heard about in movies or invented himself.

Chapter 2, Section 19

- Lying in that ditch, having just been shot at, Weary shows Billy the knife he carries.
- The knife's handle has four rings for Weary's fingers to slip through; these brass knuckles have spikes attached to them.
- Weary asks Billy how he would like to be hit be these spiked brass knuckles.
- Billy says he would prefer not to.
- Weary claims that the three-sided shape of the knife blade makes a wound that won't close.
- Weary says Billy doesn't know anything; what do they teach in college, anyway?
- Billy says he doesn't know; he was only there for six months, and it was just night school.
- Weary thinks Billy doesn't understand anything about gore. But Billy does, because on his wall at home hangs a bloodied crucifix with a detailed statue of Christ on it.

Chapter 2, Section 20

- Billy's not actually a Catholic. His father doesn't believe in anything, and his mother has been looking for the *right* church.
- Billy learned to play the organ from his mother.
- His mother never decided on a church, but she *did* develop an interest in crucifixes. She buys one in a gift shop in Santa Fe, New Mexico, which goes up on Billy's wall.

Chapter 2, Section 21

- The four men – Billy, Weary, and the two scouts – who had been sheltering in the ditch finally decide to make a run for the forest.
- The ground is covered in snow, so they leave tracks all over the place.

Chapter 2, Section 22

- Weary is carrying every piece of equipment you could possibly imagine for battle: multiple layers of clothes, a gas mask, a trench knife, a "bulletproof Bible" (2.22.2), a German phrasebook – you name it, he's got it.
- He's also got some porn of a woman attempting to have sex with a pony.
- Weary makes Billy look at this picture several times.

Chapter 2, Section 23

- Weary's picture of the lady and the pony is actually the first dirty picture in history.
- Photography was invented in 1839, by Louis J.M. Daguerre (creator of the daguerreotype. Two years later, in 1841, André le Fèvre was arrested in Paris for trying to sell pictures of a woman having sex with a pony.
- Weary buys his picture in Paris, in the same gardens (the Tuileries) where Le Fèvre was arrested for selling them a hundred years before.
- Le Fèvre's defense was that there are lots of myths of human women having sex with animals who were gods.
- Even so, Le Fèvre gets six months in jail. He dies there, of pneumonia. As you might expect: "So it goes" (2.23.4).

Chapter 2, Section 24

- Billy and the two scouts are skinny guys.
- Weary, on the other hand, is so bundled up and protected that he can imagine himself safe at home telling his true war stories.
- The irony is that Weary is still *in the middle of a war* as he's imagining his war stories.
- Here is Weary's war story: he and his anti-tank gunner buddies fight like hell against a big German attack, but everyone is killed except for Weary.
- Weary falls in with two scouts. The three shake hands all around and call themselves the

Three Musketeers.
- But then this damned college kid comes along who doesn't know what the hell he's doing. So the Three Musketeers have to help the college kid survive against all odds.
- In real life, Weary is going back to look for Billy.
- Weary can't hear anything going on around him, though, because he is caught up in his personal fantasy: an officer is congratulating the Three Musketeers and one of the scouts asks the officer to promise that wherever they are stationed next, they will be together.

Chapter 2, Section 25

- Billy has stopped in the forest, panting for breath.
- This is when he comes unstuck in time for the first time.
- Billy is transported to a time after his death – violet light and a hum – and before his birth – red light and bubbling sounds.
- Billy goes back to his life, to the moment when his father teaches him to swim at the Y.M.C.A.
- His father throws him into the deep end of the pool. Billy sinks to the bottom of the pool, and there is music everywhere.
- Billy faints, but the music goes on. He is rescued, and he resents that.

Chapter 2, Section 26

- Next, Billy jumps to 1965, when he is 41.
- He is sitting by his mother's bedside at the old age home in Pine Knoll.
- She has pneumonia and isn't expected to survive. (She does though, for years.)
- Billy's mother asks, "How ...?" (2.26.3).
- Billy asks her to finish her question.
- She says, "How did I get so *old*?" (2.26.6).

Chapter 2, Section 27

- Billy's mom loses consciousness and Billy goes into the waiting room to sit down.
- He realizes he's sitting on something – a book called *The Execution of Private Slovik*, by William Bradford Huie.
- The book tells the story of the only American soldier to be shot for cowardice since the Civil War.

- A passage from the decision on Slovik's case follows, in which the staff judge recommends that Slovik be executed, not as a punishment, but simply to maintain discipline.

Chapter 2, Section 28

- Billy zips back to 1958. He's at a Little League banquet for the team his son Robert belongs to.
- The coach of Robert's Little League team says that he would be honored just to be the team's water boy.

Chapter 2, Section 29

- Billy bounces back to 1961, to a New Year's Eve party where Billy is really, really drunk.
- He cheats on his wife (Valencia) for the first and only time, with a woman who's also very drunk, in the laundry room of the house where the party is being held.
- The woman asks Billy why he's called that.
- Billy says it was a business decision of his father's: Billy is more memorable than William; it's rare to meet a grown-up Billy; and it also makes people think he is a friend of theirs right away.

Chapter 2, Section 30

- After this whole sex thing, Billy finds himself back in his car (still ridiculously drunk) trying to find his steering wheel.
- He waves his arms around trying to locate it, but it just seems to have disappeared.
- Has the steering wheel been stolen?
- Billy passes out.
- The reason he cannot find the steering wheel is that Billy is in the *back seat* of his car.

Chapter 2, Section 31

- Billy wakes up still feeling drunk from his wild New Year's Eve – back in 1944, with Roland Weary standing over him.

- Billy tells Weary he's OK and that Weary should just leave him behind.
- Weary replies that if Billy is OK, he can't imagine what a *sick* person would look like.
- The scouts are waiting for Billy and Weary and listening to the sounds of the German soldiers looking for them.
- Weary tells the scouts that Billy may not want to live, but he's going to anyway, thanks to them, the Three Musketeers.
- This is the first time the scouts have heard of this whole Three Musketeers business.
- Billy is busy hallucinating. He imagines that, if everyone were to leave him alone, he would just turn to steam and rise into the air. He dreams that he is wearing warm socks and skating on a ballroom floor, to great applause.
- The scouts, who are experienced guys, tell Weary and Billy that they had better find someone to surrender to – because the scouts can't wait around for them anymore.
- So the two scouts leave Weary and Billy alone.

Chapter 2, Section 32

- Billy goes on skating in his imaginary sweat socks until he jumps forward in time again.
- It's the fall of 1957 and he has just been elected president of the Lions Club.
- He has to make a speech, and it's freaking him out because he has nothing prepared and his voice is very thin and high.
- But when he opens his mouth, suddenly the perfect speech comes out, in the perfect voice.
- And suddenly he is back in that frozen creek bed, with Weary about to beat him up.

Chapter 2, Section 33

- Weary is angry: he has been left behind again.
- So Weary shakes Billy. Weary thinks it's Billy's fault that the scouts have gone and Weary no longer has his imaginary "Three Musketeers."
- Billy makes noises that sound like laughter, which angers Weary even more.
- He punches Billy in the face and then kicks him in the ribs.
- Weary is about to kick Billy in the back when he looks up and sees five German soldiers and a police dog.
- The soldiers seem to wonder why one American would try to kill another here, behind enemy lines, while the victim laughs.

Chapter 3, Section 1

- The five German soldiers watching Weary and Billy fight are mopping up after the battle.
- The dog is a female German shepherd, new to war.

Chapter 3, Section 2

- Two of the Germans are kids and two are old men. They're all wearing hand-me-downs from dead soldiers.
- The fifth is their commander, a tough old soldier who has been wounded four times and then sent back to war.
- The commander's boots are pretty much the only thing he owns; he believes that if you look deeply enough into the polish on them, you can see Adam and Eve.
- Billy looks deep into the German commander's boots and sees Adam and Eve.

Chapter 3, Section 3

- Next to the commander's feet are a second pair of feet in hinged wooden clogs.
- They belong to one of the boys in the German squad.
- He has the face of an angel.

Chapter 3, Section 4

- The boy with the face of an angel helps Billy out of the snow and searches him for weapons.
- Three shots ring out: the two American scouts who left Billy and Weary behind have just been shot by the Germans.
- The commander gives the beautiful boy Weary's pistol and his excellent boots. He hands the rest of Weary's gear (including the dirty picture) to the other men in his squad.
- Weary has to wear the boy's wooden clogs, which make his feet bleed.
- Weary and Billy are marched to a place where prisoners of war are being held.
- Billy falls asleep on the shoulder of a captain, who is both a rabbi and a chaplain. The rabbi's hand has been shot.
- Billy wakes up having traveled through time.
- He is in the middle of examining a female patient with his optometry machine.
- He can't remember how old he is or what year it is.

- The patient asks Billy if he sees anything wrong with her eyes.
- He says no, she just needs glasses for reading.

Chapter 3, Section 5

- The patient leaves Billy's optometry office.
- He looks out the window and sees his Cadillac parked outside.
- The date on the license plate is 1967.
- Billy is forty-four years old.

Chapter 3, Section 6

- Billy looks at his desk, where he finds an optometry magazine.
- A siren goes off, startling Billy.
- Billy worries about the start of World War III.
- He closes his eyes and finds himself back in World War II, leaning on the shoulder of the wounded rabbi.

Chapter 3, Section 7

- The American prisoners of war start marching out on the road again.
- A German reporter takes pictures of Billy and Weary's feet as proof that Americans aren't so well-equipped after all.
- Billy and several German soldiers stage Billy's capture for the reporter's camera.

Chapter 3, Section 8

- As Billy is staging his capture for the German cameras, 1944 is fading away into 1967.
- Billy is on his way to a Lions Club meeting.
- He stops at a red light in a mostly African-American neighborhood in Ilium, New York.
- The people who live there hate the neighborhood so much that they burned it down the month before.
- The ruins of this ghetto remind Billy of towns he saw during the war.

Chapter 3, Section 9

- An African-American man taps on Billy's car window.
- The traffic light changes and Billy drives on.

Chapter 3, Section 10

- Billy drives past a construction site where his old house used to be.
- It's OK that this new development is going up, thinks Billy.

Chapter 3, Section 11

- The speaker at the Lions Club meeting is a Marine major who has fought two tours in Vietnam.
- The speaker thinks that the U.S. should increase bombings of North Vietnam.

Chapter 3, Section 12

- Billy does not protest the bombing of North Vietnam, despite the horrible things he has seen bombings do.
- He is just having lunch at the Lions Club.

Chapter 3, Section 13

- There is a prayer hanging on the wall of Billy's office that says, "God grant me the serenity to accept the things I cannot change, courage to change the things I can, and wisdom always to tell the difference" (3.13.1).
- Among the (many) things Billy cannot change are the past, the present, and the future.

Chapter 3, Section 14

- Someone introduces Billy to the Marine major at the Lions club, telling the major that Billy is a veteran and that his son is with the Green Berets in Vietnam.
- The Marine major tells Billy that he should be very proud of his son.
- Billy answers that he certainly is proud.

Chapter 3, Section 15

- Billy goes home for a nap after lunch.
- His doctor has told Billy he must nap every day.
- This prescription is supposed to cure Billy of a secret problem: every now and then, for no obvious reason, Billy starts to cry.
- No one knows about this quiet weeping except for Billy and his doctor.

Chapter 3, Section 16

- Billy owns a beautiful house and makes lots of money at his optometry business.
- He also owns part shares in a Holiday Inn and three Tastee-Freeze stands.

Chapter 3, Section 17

- Billy's home is empty.
- His daughter is about to get married and she and Billy's wife have gone downtown to pick patterns for her wedding silverware.
- Billy has no servants and no dog.
- There used to be a dog (Spot), but he died.

Chapter 3, Section 18

- Billy goes into his bedroom.
- He has an electric blanked and a mattress with a massage setting ("The Magic Fingers").
- Billy gets undressed and lies down in bed, but he cannot sleep.
- He turns on the Magic Fingers and the bed vibrates as he weeps.

Chapter 3, Section 19

- The doorbell rings and Billy goes to see who it is.
- There is a man at the door having some kind of seizure.
- Billy also sees another man across the street ringing doorbells. This man has one leg and is on crutches.
- Billy realizes that these two men are selling subscriptions for magazines that will never come; it's a con Billy has been warned about at his Lions Club meetings.
- Billy spots a guy sitting in a Buick watching the two men selling their subscriptions. Billy realizes that this is the guy who hired them for the con.
- Billy blinks, and when he opens his eyes, he is back in Luxembourg, a prisoner of war.

Chapter 3, Section 20

- Billy is marching with the other American prisoners of war, with his hands on top of his head.
- He keeps running into Weary, who is also crying.
- Weary is crying from pain because his feet ache so badly from the wooden clogs the German commander made him wear.
- At each fork in the road, more American soldiers join the line of prisoners of war.

Chapter 3, Section 21

- The prisoners of war march down a road that's also carrying trucks full of German soldiers to the front.
- One of the German soldiers spits at the Americans.
- His spit hits Roland Weary.

Chapter 3, Section 22

- Billy keeps bumping into Weary.
- Weary keeps begging Billy to "Walk right!" (3.22.3) and not bump into him because his feet are so sore.
- The American soldiers cross from Luxembourg into Germany. (The Battle of the Bulge, at

which these guys were captured, was a German military campaign from southern Belgium into Luxembourg.

Chapter 3, Section 23

- At the Luxembourg/German border, there is a movie camera set up to film the Germans' successes.
- The cameramen focus on Billy's face for a moment before shifting to the distance and the battleground.
- The prisoners of war get onto a train taking them to the interior of Germany.

Chapter 3, Section 24

- A squad of captive American colonels waits near Billy.
- One of them is very sick and mistakes Billy for a member of his own squadron.
- He asks Billy which regiment he belongs to.
- Billy can't remember.

Chapter 3, Section 25

- The colonel yells, "It's me, boys! It's Wild Bob!" (3.25.1).
- The colonel has always wanted his troops to call him Wild Bob.
- Wild Bob is so sick that he imagines he is talking to his troops.
- Weary is actually a member of Wild Bob's regiment, but his feet hurt so much that he pays no attention to Wild Bob's words.
- Wild Bob tells his (imagined) troops that after the war, they are going to have a reunion in his hometown of Cody, Wyoming.
- Looking straight at Billy, Wild Bob says, "If you're ever in Cody, Wyoming, just ask for Wild Bob!" (3.25.5).
- The narrator tells us he has been to Cody.
- So has his friend, Bernard V. O'Hare.

Chapter 3, Section 26

- Billy and Weary are separated into different cars on the same train.
- German soldiers are writing the number of prisoners on each train car on the side of the train, along with their nationalities.
- Most of the guys in Billy's car are very young, but there's one forty-year-old private.
- The private used to be a hobo, and he tells Billy that this train car isn't so bad.

Chapter 3, Section 27

- A man in a boxcar near Billy's yells to the guards that a soldier has died in their car.
- The four guards nod and don't open the door of the boxcar.
- Instead, they open the door to the car next to Billy's, which has food, bunk beds, and a stove.
- The four guards go inside and close the door.
- Eventually, they come out smoking and speaking to each other.
- The Americans across the way tell the guards about the dead man.
- The guards remove the dead man from the box car.
- It's Wild Bob.

Chapter 3, Section 28

- A fleet of trains take off carrying prisoners of war.
- The trains are all painted with orange and black stripes to indicate to the enemy air force that they shouldn't be bombed; they are carrying prisoners of war.

Chapter 3, Section 29

- The war is coming to an end.
- These trains are carrying POWs in late December 1944, and the war will end in May 1945.
- There is nothing left to eat and no fuel to keep the POWs warm, yet the Germans keep taking prisoners.

Chapter 3, Section 30

- Billy's train does not move for two days.
- The former hobo tells Billy that their current situation ain't bad.
- A train passes Billy's train and whistles; Billy's train whistles back.

Chapter 3, Section 31

- The train is not moving.
- Guards patrol up and down past the boxcars, passing food and water into the locked cars.
- The prisoners are using their helmets as toilets.
- Billy is one of the "dumpers" (3.28.2): he disposes of the excrement through a ventilator in the boxcar.

Chapter 3, Section 32

- The prisoners in the train cars take turns standing and lying down.
- The train finally starts to move east, further into Germany.
- Billy spends Christmas night lying "nestled like spoons" (3.29.3) next to the former hobo.
- Billy travels forward in time to 1967, the night when he is kidnapped by the Tralfamadorians.

Chapter 4, Section 1

- It's his daughter Barbara's wedding night, and Billy can't sleep.
- He and Valencia are lying "nestled like spoons" (4.1.2); she is sleeping soundly.
- Billy gets out of bed.
- He looks down at his bare feet, which are ivory and blue.

Chapter 4, Section 2

- Billy goes upstairs, knowing that he is about to be taken by aliens.
- He goes past the empty rooms of his children, all grown up now.
- Billy enters his daughter's room, where her telephone is still hooked up to the wall.

- The phone rings: it's a wrong number.

Chapter 4, Section 3

- Billy goes downstairs to the kitchen, where there is a leftover bottle of champagne from his daughter's wedding reception.
- Billy pops open the bottle, but the champagne has gone flat.
- He knows he's got about half an hour to kill before the aliens come.
- He comes unstuck from time just enough to watch a movie about World War II.
- Because the film is running backwards, it starts with the ruins of a city and ends with everything shiny and new.

Chapter 4, Section 4

- The movie keeps going backwards: the bombers return to the United States and all their weapons are removed.
- The pilots take off their uniforms and go back to being school kids.
- Billy assumes that even Hitler goes back to being a baby.
- Everyone in the whole world turns back into a baby.
- In fact, all of creation moves backwards until they arrive at Adam and Eve.

Chapter 4, Section 5

- Billy goes outside to wait for a flying saucer.
- He hears a flying saucer from Tralfamadore coming for him. It sounds like an owl hooting.
- A dog barks.

Chapter 4, Section 6

- The Tralfamadorian saucer is a hundred feet wide, with portholes and purple lights.
- It lowers a ladder to Billy, which he has to climb because there is a "zap gun" (4.6.2) aimed at him.

Chapter 4, Section 7

- The Tralfamadorians do not have voice boxes, so they cannot speak aloud.
- They communicate using their minds, talking to Billy via a computer that synthesizes speech.
- They tell him that both he and they are like bugs trapped in amber.
- There is no *why*, there is only what *is*.

Chapter 4, Section 8

- The Tralfamadorians knock Billy out and put him in the hold of their flying saucer.
- Billy is thrown out of time.
- When he wakes up, he is in the boxcar with other prisoners of war, on his way deeper into Germany.

Chapter 4, Section 9

- Billy slowly lies down.
- He knows that he has to make himself as invisible as possible.
- The reason why soon becomes clear: when a prisoner of war notices that it is *Billy* near him, he demands that Billy get up and go away.
- The prisoner of war makes a lot of ruckus and wakes the other prisoners.
- They tell him he has to sleep somewhere else because he yells, kicks, and whimpers in his sleep.
- Everyone in the car tells Billy to keep the hell away.

Chapter 4, Section 10

- Billy has to sleep standing up, or not at all.
- It's getting colder and colder, and the guards stop feeding them.

Chapter 4, Section 11

- On the eighth day, the former hobo tells Billy this experience isn't so bad.
- On the ninth day, the former hobo dies.
- In the car next to Billy's, Weary also dies on the ninth day, from gangrene due to his ruined feet.
- Weary tells everyone in his car that it's Billy Pilgrim's fault that he's dying.

Chapter 4, Section 12

- On the tenth day, the door to Billy's car opens.
- Billy coughs and "shit[s] thin gruel" (4.12.1).
- This proves Newton's Third Law of Motion: every action demands an equal and opposite reaction.

Chapter 4, Section 13

- Billy's train arrives at a prison.
- The guards coo like owls at the prisoners in an effort to get them to move without struggling.

Chapter 4, Section 14

- Billy is the second-to-last prisoner to exit his car.
- The last prisoner in the car is the dead former hobo.

Chapter 4, Section 15

- Billy doesn't want to jump from the train car to the ground, so the guards help him down.
- As the train has crossed through Germany and dropped off its prisoners at different prisons, the number of cars has gotten smaller and smaller. Now the entire train consists of one engine and three boxcars.
- One of the boxcars is the car with the bunk beds and food for the guards.

Chapter 4, Section 16

- The prisoners are ushered past three huge piles of overcoats, which belonged to prisoners who have died.
- The German guards want each of the prisoners without an overcoat to take one.
- Billy takes a coat that is small and disgusting. He notices that his fellow soldiers all have soldiers' coats; he is the only one with a civilian's coat.
- Billy and the other prisoners are marched toward the long, narrow sheds where they are being kept.

Chapter 4, Section 17

- Billy sees his first Russian on the other side of a barbed wire fence.
- The Russian's face looks at Billy's hopefully, as though Billy is bringing him good news.
- Billy blacks out and then comes to in a delousing station at the prison.
- He takes off his clothes when the Germans order him to, just like he does when he gets to Tralfamadore.
- The Germans comment on how weak Billy looks.

Chapter 4, Section 18

- One of the better American bodies belongs to a high school teacher from Indiana named Edgar Derby.
- Derby is in Weary's car when Weary dies.
- He is old enough to have a son in the war as well.
- Derby's son will survive the war, but Derby will be killed by a firing squad in 68 days.
- The worst body is not Billy's. It belongs to a car thief from Illinois named Paul Lazzaro.
- Lazzaro has promised a dying Weary that he will find some way to get revenge on Billy for Weary's death.
- Lazzaro looks at all the naked American soldiers and wonders which one is Billy.

Chapter 4, Section 19

- The prisoners are all showered with cold water.

- Their clothes are taken away to be fumigated with poison gas.
- Lice and fleas and bacteria die by the billions.
- Billy travels back to the time of his babyhood, when his mother has just given him a bath.

Chapter 4, Section 20

- Billy is an optometrist again.
- He is playing golf and doing pretty well.
- He has a spell of dizziness, and when he comes out of it, he is strapped to a yellow chair in a white room on a flying saucer on the way to Tralfamadore.

Chapter 4, Section 21

- Billy asks where he is.
- A Tralfamadorian replies that Billy is caught in another moment in which he is on his way to Tralfamadore.
- There is no place for explanation, it adds: in each moment, we are like bugs caught in amber. We simply are.
- Billy tells it that it doesn't seem to believe in free will.

Chapter 4, Section 22

- The Tralfamadorian answers that, no, it doesn't.
- In fact, of all the inhabited planets in the universe that it has visited, no one believes in free will except for Earthlings.

Chapter 5, Section 1

- According to the Tralfamadorians, the stars don't look like points of light. They look like streaks, because the Tralfamadorians can see where the stars began and where they are going.
- People look like multi-legged creatures with baby legs at one end and old people's legs on the other.

Chapter 5, Section 2

- Billy wants something to read on his way to Tralfamadore.
- The only book they have in English is *Valley of the Dolls*, by Jacqueline Susann).
- Billy thinks it's OK, but he doesn't want to read only one book.
- He asks if there's anything else, and gets a selection of Tralfamadorian novels.
- They're all tiny.

Chapter 5, Section 3

- Billy can't read Tralfamadorian, but he does see how the books are laid out: in short sections separated by stars.
- Billy says that the stars seem like telegrams.
- The Tralfamadorian says it's true: the stars are short messages describing a situation or scene.
- The Tralfamadorians read these messages all at once to get a complete, beautiful scene.
- There is no beginning, middle, end, or moral in a Tralfamadorian novel.

Chapter 5, Section 4

- Billy is thrown back to his childhood, when he was on a trip to the Grand Canyon with his family.
- His father feels that it's been worth the awful drive to see the Canyon at last.
- Billy is totally terrified that he's going to fall in, and he wets his pants.

Chapter 5, Section 5

- During this trip to the Grand Canyon, another tourist asks a park ranger if many people kill themselves by jumping in.
- The ranger says yes, around three people a year.

Chapter 5, Section 6

- Billy jumps forward about ten days in time, to a visit with his family to Carlsbad Caverns in New Mexico.
- When he's inside the caverns, a park ranger turns out the lanterns for a moment so that the tourists can experience total darkness.
- Billy can't see anything at all: he loses track of whether he's still alive or not.
- Then Billy catches a glimpse of his father's lighted watch dial.

Chapter 5, Section 7

- Billy finds himself back in the war.
- He gets his deloused clothes back. His coat, taken from a pile of coats belonging to dead men, is full of bullet holes.
- The coat is so small on Billy that it splits up the back and the sleeves come off, leaving him with a fur-collared vest instead of a coat.
- The Germans laugh their asses off at this sight.

Chapter 5, Section 8

- The Germans put the Americans into groups of five to march through the camp.
- They see more starving Russians behind barbed wire fences.
- They come to a shed where a man takes down their names.
- This gives them the legal status of "alive" – before, they were all M.I.A. and presumed dead.

Chapter 5, Section 9

- As the prisoners march, one of the guards overhears an American saying something he does not like.
- He pulls the American out of line and knocks him down.
- The American is totally surprised – he had meant no harm and didn't think the guard would understand.
- He asks, why him?
- The guard answers: Why you? Why anyone?

Chapter 5, Section 10

- Billy gets a dog tag with his prisoner number on it.
- The dog tag is perforated in the middle so it can be snapped in half.
- If Billy dies, half the tag would stay attached to his body and the other half would mark his grave.
- After Edgar Derby gets shot later on, a doctor snaps his dog tag in two.

Chapter 5, Section 11

- Now that the Americans have all been tagged, the Red Cross will be able to inform their families that they are (a) prisoners, and (b) still alive.
- Billy is walking next to Paul Lazzaro, who promised Weary he would get revenge on Billy for Weary's death.
- Next to Lazzaro is Edgar Derby, who will be shot at the end of the war.
- A guard tells them to halt.
- They stop outside a long shed with tin chimneys, which are giving off smoke.
- The door to the shed opens and the prisoners hear English voices singing "Hail, Hail, the Gang's All Here" from Gilbert and Sullivan's light opera *The Pirates of Penzance*.

Chapter 5, Section 12

- The guys who are serenading the new prisoners are English, the first English-speaking prisoners taken in the war. They've been in this camp for years.
- They're all officers, and they have all tried to escape from other prisons at least once.
- They can't break out of this one, though, because there's nowhere to go: the POW barracks are surrounded by camps of starving Russians. Even if they managed to tunnel out of their own prison, they would just wind up in another one.
- The Englishmen are in great physical shape: they've basically been spending the last four years working out and eating Red Cross rations.
- Thanks to a bureaucratic error, the English soldiers have been getting extra food and supplies that are keeping them better fed than pretty much anyone else in Europe during the war.

Chapter 5, Section 13

- The Germans love these English officers because they are exactly what Germans expect English officers to be like.
- The English have known about the new group of American prisoners joining them for long enough to spruce up the camp and make it look nice for the new guys. (Seriously.)
- They welcome the Americans with open arms and keeping talking about "Jerry" being on the run.
- Billy doesn't know who "Jerry" is. In case you're wondering, it's an English slang term for Germans.

Chapter 5, Section 14

- Billy is inside next to a stove with many kettles on it.
- There is a table set as though for a feast.
- Each place setting has a safety razor, a washcloth, chocolate, two cigars, a bar of soap, ten cigarettes, a book of matches, a pencil, and a candle next to it.
- Only the candles and the soap come from the Germans.
- The English officers have no way of knowing that the candles and soap have been made from the rendered fat of Jews, Gypsies, gay people, and Communists murdered in the Nazi concentration camps.

Chapter 5, Section 15

- The banquet hall the English have set up is filled with butter, fresh bread, marmalade, sliced beef, soup, scrambled eggs – a real feast.
- Billy sees a stage set up at the end of the shed: it's got two thrones, a bucket, a mop, and a giant clock.
- This is where a musical version of *Cinderella* will be performed at the end of the night.

Chapter 5, Section 16

- Billy has been standing too close to the hot stove, and the hem of his tiny coat catches on fire.
- It's not burning very quickly, at least.
- Billy wishes there were a phone he could use to call his mother and tell her that he's alive

and well.

Chapter 5, Section 17

- The Englishmen are totally surprised at the sight of the filthy people who have appeared in their camp.
- One of the Englishmen sees that Billy is on fire and puts him out.
- When Billy doesn't say anything, an Englishman asks if Billy can talk and/or hear.
- Billy nods.
- The Englishman is filled with pity: he says Billy's not a man, he's a broken kite.
- The Englishman asks if Billy is really an American.
- Billy says yes, he is a private. He doesn't remember what has happened to his boots.
- The Englishman is shocked by Billy's coat. He tells Billy that the coat is an *insult*. The Englishman says Billy shouldn't let the Germans humiliate him like that.
- Billy faints.
- He comes to realizing that he has eaten, and he's sitting and facing the stage where *Cinderella* is being performed.
- Billy laughs hysterically, so hard that his laughs turn to screams.
- They carry him to a neighboring shed, which has a hospital. There are no other patients there.

Chapter 5, Section 18

- Billy has been put in a bed and left with an American volunteer to look after him.
- The American is the high school teacher who will be shot in Dresden.
- Derby sits reading Stephen Crane's *Red Badge of Courage* while Billy floats in morphine dreams.

Chapter 5, Section 19

- In Billy's morphine dreams, he sees giraffes in a garden.
- He is also a giraffe.
- The giraffes accept Billy as one of their own.
- Two giraffes approach Billy.
- They are female giraffes and they kiss him with their mobile lips.
- Why?

Chapter 5, Section 20

- Billy travels in time to Spring 1948, when he lies in a ward for nonviolent mental patients in a V.A. hospital in Lake Placid, New York.
- The birds are singing outside his window: "Poo-tee-weet?"
- Billy has committed himself to the hospital because of a breakdown in his final year at the Ilium School of Optometry.
- His doctors think he's going crazy because Billy's father had thrown him into the deep end of the Y.M.C.A. swimming pool and then taken him to the rim of the Grand Canyon. It can't be because of the war.
- The man next to Bill is a former infantry captain and current drunk, Eliot Rosewater.
- Rosewater introduces Billy to science fiction, specifically the works of (fictional) author Kilgore Trout.
- Science fiction becomes the only thing Billy can read, and Kilgore Trout his favorite author.
- Both Rosewater and Billy find life meaningless because of experiences they have had in the War. They're trying to reinvent their universes, and science fiction helps.

Chapter 5, Section 21

- Rosewater says that everything there is to know about life is in Feodor (a.k.a. Fyodor) Dostoevsky's novel *The Brothers Karamazov*.
- But knowing everything there is to know about life isn't *enough* anymore.

Chapter 5, Section 22

- Rosewater tells a psychiatrist that they need a *new* set of lies or else people aren't going to want to go on living.

Chapter 5, Section 23

- Next to Billy's bed are two pills, an ashtray with three cigarettes, and a glass of water.
- The cigarettes belong to Billy's mother, who has headed to the bathroom.
- Billy covers his head with a blanket whenever his mother comes to see him at the mental hospital.

- She upsets him because she is his mother: she has gone to so much trouble to give Billy life, but Billy doesn't even *like* life.

Chapter 5, Section 24

- Billy hears Eliot Rosewater come in and lie down on his bed.
- Billy's mother comes in and sits down next to Billy's bed.
- Rosewater greets Billy's mother. Rosewater is trying to be really sympathetic with everyone he meets to see if it will make the world a better place.
- Billy's mother tells Rosewater that one day, when she is there, Billy is going to uncover his head and say, "Hello, Mom...Gee, it's good to see you, Mom. How have you been?" (5.24.5).
- Billy's mother says she prays for that every night. She then asks Rosewater if his mother comes to see him often.
- She doesn't: Rosewater's mother is dead. Still, Rosewater says, his mother had a happy life while it lasted.
- Billy's mother tells Rosewater that Billy's father is dead.
- And it goes on and on, this empty duet between the two.

Chapter 5, Section 25

- Maybe Billy's been working too hard, Rosewater tells Billy's mother.
- Rosewater is in the middle of a Kilgore Trout novel called *Maniacs in the Fourth Dimension* .
- Kilgore Trout claims that there really are vampires and werewolves and heaven and hell, but we can't see them. They're in the fourth dimension and we humans can only see in three.

Chapter 5, Section 26

- Billy's mother tells Rosewater that Billy is engaged to a rich girl, which is some comfort.
- Billy falls asleep under his blanket.
- When he wakes up, he's back at the prison with Edgar Derby reading next to his bed.
- Billy thinks of his memory of Edgar Derby getting shot by a firing squad at the end of the war.

Chapter 5, Section 27

- The head Englishman, a colonel captured at the Battle of Dunkirk, comes in to check on Billy.
- Edgar Derby says Billy's still alive, but dead to the world – in other words, unconscious.
- The colonel says it must be nice to be alive but feel nothing.
- The colonel then tells Derby that Derby and Billy are the only two American prisoners who haven't shaved yet.
- When the colonel sees the American prisoners with clean-shaven faces, he thinks they all seem really young: like they're in the Children's Crusade.
- The two men continue their conversation, which amounts to: a lot of troops are being injured and killed.
- Derby and his men surrendered to the Germans to avoid being killed.

Chapter 5, Section 28

- Billy returns to the veteran's hospital.
- From under his blanket, he asks if his mother is gone.
- A voice answers, "yes."
- The voice belongs to Billy's fiancée Valencia, a very large young woman wearing a diamond ring that Billy found in Germany.
- Billy doesn't want to marry Valencia and thinks the fact that he has asked her to marry him is proof that he's going crazy.

Chapter 5, Section 29

- Billy greets Valencia.
- Valencia asks Billy if he wants some candy and if he's OK.
- Billy answers that he's feeling much better. He asks Valencia to tell the people at the optometry school that he says hello.
- Valencia promises she will.

Chapter 5, Section 30

- Valencia asks if Billy wants her to bring him any books.
- Billy says he's got plenty – he has access to Rosewater's science fiction collection.
- Billy asks Rosewater (who's sitting in the next bed) what he's reading.
- It's another Kilgore Trout novel: *The Gospel of Outer Space*.
- The hero of the novel is an alien (who looks like a Tralfamadorian) who wants to know how Christians can be so cruel.
- He decides that the problem is the New Testament. It's supposed to teach people to be merciful, but what it actually seems to teach is: "Before you kill somebody, make absolutely sure he isn't well-connected" (5.30.7).

Chapter 5, Section 31

- The visitor from space comes to this "well-connected" message in this way:
- Christ, as a human being, doesn't look like much. But he's the Son of the Most Powerful Being in the Universe.
- So, when Christ is crucified, readers think: "Uh oh! They sure picked the *wrong* guy to lynch!"
- But is there a *right* (or at least, *less wrong*) person to lynch?
- The message the Gospels seem to teach is that there are *right* people to lynch: people who are not well-connected.

Chapter 5, Section 32

- So, in this Kilgore Trout novel, the alien gives the people of Earth the gift of a new gospel.
- In this gospel, Jesus still says all of the beautiful things he says in the other gospels, but he's a nobody; he's not the son of God.
- So one day, a group of people crucify him and they think they aren't going to be punished for it because he's a nobody.
- But then, just before Christ dies, the voice of God sounds out.
- He tells the Earth that he is *adopting* this nobody, that from now on, Jesus is the Son of the Creator of the Universe forever.
- And God promises: "From this moment on, He will punish horribly anybody who torments a bum who has no connections" (5.32.3).

Chapter 5, Section 33

- Valencia is still sitting by Billy's hospital bed eating chocolate.
- Rosewater throws Kilgore Trout's novel under his bed.
- Rosewater loves Trout's *ideas*, but hates that Trout can't write worth a damn.

Chapter 5, Section 34

- Rosewater continues: Trout writes about people of Earth all the time, but they all sound like Americans.
- No one knows where Trout lives. All of his books are published by different publishing houses, and no one seems to have heard of him except Rosewater.
- Rosewater compliments Valencia on her engagement ring.

Chapter 5, Section 35

- It turns out that Kilgore Trout lives in Ilium, New York – Billy's hometown.

Chapter 5, Section 36

- Valencia asks Billy to help her make a decision about their silver pattern.
- She doesn't want them to *rush* into the choice: they have to live with this pattern for the rest of their lives.

Chapter 5, Section 37

- Billy is forty-four years old, on the planet Tralfamadore, sitting naked in their zoo.
- He knows that he cannot escape: the atmosphere outside his habitat is filled with cyanide, and Earth is 446,120,000,000,000,000 miles away.

Chapter 5, Section 38

- Billy's habitat is mostly made up of Sears furniture stolen from Iowa City.
- He has a record player (which works) and a television (which doesn't).
- There is nowhere in his habitat where he can hide from the Tralfamadorians who come to see him – not even in the bathroom.

Chapter 5, Section 39

- Billy brushes his teeth and goes into his kitchen.
- There is a picture painted on the door of the refrigerator of a couple riding a tandem bicycle in the 1890s.
- Billy can't imagine anything at all about this couple.

Chapter 5, Section 40

- Billy eats well out of cans. He also keeps himself fit, as he was taught to in the Army.
- The Tralfamadorians don't know that Billy isn't good-looking by human standards. This does good things for Billy's confidence.
- One of the Tralfamadorians asks Billy (via a speaker in his habitat) if he's happy there.
- Billy answers that he's about as happy on Tralfamadore as he was on Earth.

Chapter 5, Section 41

- The Tralfamadorians have five sexes that are all necessary to make babies.
- They all look the same to Billy, though, because their sexual differences are in the fourth dimension.
- The Tralfamadorians tell Billy that they have observed seven sex differences in Earth humans.
- Billy has absolutely no idea what five of those seven sex differences could be, since they're in the fourth dimension.
- The Tralfamadorians try to explain, but Billy doesn't get it.

Chapter 5, Section 42

- The Tralfamadorians don't get Billy either: they can't imagine how humans see time.
- They keep making up huge, ridiculous metaphors to explain how restricted human sight is.

Chapter 5, Section 43

- Billy thinks the Tralfamadorians will be freaked out by how much murder there is on Earth.
- Billy has been reading a lot of science fiction and thinks aliens will be concerned about Earth's warlike nature and advancing weaponry.
- So he asks the Tralfamadorians, using some of his own war experiences, how a planet can live in peace.
- The Tralfamadorians clearly think Billy is being stupid.
- The Tralfamadorians tell Billy that they know how the Universe is going to end, and it has nothing to do with Earth. A Tralfamadorian experimenting with new fuels will press a button and the Universe will disappear.

Chapter 5, Section 44

- But if the Tralfamadorians know how the Universe is going to end, why don't they *stop it*, asks Billy.
- The Tralfamadorians reply that the moment is structured that way: the pilot has always pressed the button, and he always will.

Chapter 5, Section 45

- Billy asks if preventing war on Earth is equally pointless.
- Yes, the Tralfamadorians answer. What the Tralfamadorians do is, they concentrate on the pleasant moments. They have had terrible wars, but they ignore them.
- Billy goes to sleep and travels in time to his wedding night with Valencia.
- Billy and Valencia are going to conceive their son, Robert Pilgrim, this night.
- While Billy is making love with Valencia, she is imagining that she is Queen Elizabeth I of England, while Billy is supposed to be Christopher Columbus (not historically possible, but who are we to stop the lady from her role-playing?).

Chapter 5, Section 46

- Billy has an orgasm, thus doing his part to produce his son, Robert. Of course, according to the Tralfamadorians, Robert has seven parents.
- Billy is rich now: because he has married a girl no one else would marry, his father-in-law has given him a new Buick and has made him the manager of his Ilium Optometry office.
- Billy's mother says that the Pilgrim family is moving up in the world.

Chapter 5, Section 47

- Billy's honeymoon is taking place in New England, in the heat of the late summer.
- Valencia thanks Billy and begins to cry. She says she's crying because she's so happy: she thought no one would marry her.

Chapter 5, Section 48

- Valencia promises Billy she's going to lose weight and become beautiful for him.
- Billy says it's OK. He thinks to himself that he's time-traveled through most of their marriage, and he knows it's going to be tolerable all the way through.

Chapter 5, Section 49

- A yacht sails past Billy and Valencia's suite.
- Two beautiful people are standing on the Yacht: Lance Rumfoord and Cynthia Landry, who are honeymooning, too.
- Oddly, Billy would later share a hospital room with Lance Rumfoord's uncle, who is the official historian of the United States Air Force.

Chapter 5, Section 50

- Valencia associates sex and glamour with war.
- She asks Billy if he ever thinks about the war and lays her hand on his thigh.

Chapter 5, Section 51

- Valencia thinks Billy is full of secrets that he doesn't want to talk about. (He is, of course: Tralfamadore, time-traveling, and so on.)
- Billy has a great idea for what should be written on his tombstone. On the next page, there is an illustration of a tombstone with the words, "Everything Was Beautiful, and Nothing Hurt" (5.51).
- Valencia tells him that she once overheard Billy telling her father about the execution of Edgar Derby.
- Billy had to bury Derby after he was shot.
- Derby didn't really seem scared; they had given him drugs to keep him calm in front of the firing squad.
- Billy excuses himself to go to the bathroom and winds up back in 1944.

Chapter 5, Section 52

- Back in the prison hospital, Billy is lying in bed and Edgar Derby has fallen asleep.
- Billy gets out of bed and sneaks out, still high as a kite on morphine.
- Billy gets caught in a barbed-wire fence and can't get free.
- A Russian prisoner on the other side of the fence sees Billy tangled up and asks what country he's from.
- The Russian untangles Billy, who wanders off into the dark.
- The Russian waves and says good-bye.

Chapter 5, Section 53

- Billy is confused and starts wondering where he should go next.
- He hears someone crying and goes toward the sound. He's approaching one of the camp toilets.
- On the latrine wall he sees a beautifully painted sign: "Please Leave This Latrine As Tidy As You Found It" (5.53.5).
- The crying is coming from inside the latrine. All of the American soldiers have diarrhea thanks to the rich food the English officers gave them at the feast.
- One of the crying Americans is the author of this very book.
- Billy staggers away from the latrine and toward the prison hospital.
- He goes through the hospital door and back into his honeymoon.
- Valencia says she has missed him.

Chapter 5, Section 54

- Billy goes to sleep with Valencia and travels back in time to 1944, to his trip from South Carolina to his father's funeral in upstate New York.
- He travels by train. When he reaches Ilium, New York, the porter wakes him from a deep sleep.
- The porter tells Billy he had a huge erection while he was sleeping.

Chapter 5, Section 55

- During Billy's morphine-addled night in the prison hospital, the English officers bring in another American soldier.
- The American is Paul Lazzaro, the Illinois car thief, whose arm has been broken by an Englishman whose cigarettes he tried to steal.
- The Englishman Lazzaro tried to rob played Cinderella's Blue Fairy Godmother in the play they put on to welcome the Americans.
- The Blue Fairy Godmother is carrying Lazzaro's upper body; the British colonel who gave Billy his morphine is carrying his feet.
- The two men agree that the Americans seem like a pathetic bunch.
- A German army major comes by the hospital to apologize to the Englishmen for having to put up with the Americans.
- He promises the English (whom he likes very much) that the Americans are going to be shipped off to Dresden in a couple days.
- The German major is carrying an essay written by an American turned Nazi about the behavior of American prisoners of war.
- The author of this (fictional) essay is named Howard W. Campbell, Jr., and he will hang himself at the end of the war.

Chapter 5, Section 56

- The British colonel sets Paul Lazzaro's broken arm.
- The German major reads aloud from war criminal Howard W. Campbell Jr.'s essay on American prisoners of war.
- Campbell claims that the poor in America are unique in the world for hating themselves and loving the rich.
- The motto of the States, Campbell says, is: "If you're so smart, why ain't you rich?"

(5.56.2).

Chapter 5, Section 57

- Howard W. Campbell Jr. continues: Americans believe that it is (or *should be*) easy for anyone to make money. So, when they *can't* make any money (because money is hard to come by), they only blame themselves.
- Campbell claims that the nasty behavior of American prisoners of war in German prisons comes from the fact that the poor in America hate themselves so much.

Chapter 5, Section 58

- Campbell's essay goes on to say that the hatred Americans have for their poor is clear even in their army uniforms, which look like ill-fitting business suits.
- Campbell's essay warns that Germans may find that American soldiers all behave like "sulky children" (5.58.3).
- Billy goes to sleep and wakes up to find his daughter Barbara yelling at him for writing letters about Tralfamadore to the newspapers.

Chapter 5, Section 59

- It's 1968, and Barbara Pilgrim warns Billy that, if he keeps acting like a child, she is going to treat him like a child.
- Barbara also says that it's freezing in his house: the furnace isn't working. Billy says he hadn't noticed.
- Barbara shouts that, if they leave Billy alone, he'll freeze or starve to death.
- Barbara is enjoying depriving Billy of his dignity in the name of daughterly love.

Chapter 5, Section 60

- Barbara makes Billy go to bed until the oil-burner man can come by to fix the furnace.
- Billy lies in bed and travels in time to the zoo on Tralfamadore, where the Tralfamadorians have just brought him a mate: movie star Montana Wildhack.

Chapter 5, Section 61

- Montana has been drugged.
- The Tralfamadorians bring her in to Billy's habitat and leave her on his lounge chair.
- There is a huge crowd outside: all the Tralfamadorians want to see the Earthlings have sex.

Chapter 5, Section 62

- Montana wakes up slowly, and Billy tells her not to be afraid.
- The last thing Montana remembers is lying in the sun next to her swimming pool in Palm Springs.
- She turns her head to see the Tralfamadorians lined up outside their habitat. She screams.

Chapter 5, Section 63

- The Tralfamadorians are a little freaked out by Montana's screaming.
- The zookeeper orders the Earthling habitat dome to be covered with a cloth. Under the cloth, Billy switches on a light.
- The shadows remind Billy of the amazing architecture of Dresden before it was bombed.

Chapter 5, Section 64

- Montana slowly comes to love Billy. (And by slowly, we mean a week.)
- Billy doesn't sleep with her until she reassures him that she *wants* him to.
- He time-travels from the bed he shares with Montana to his bed in Ilium, New York, in 1968.
- The oil-burner man has fixed the furnace.
- Billy's bed smells: he's had a wet dream about Montana Wildhack.

Chapter 5, Section 65

- Billy goes back to his optometry office the next morning.
- His assistants are surprised to see him because Barbara has told them that Billy might never practice again.
- He looks at the eyes of a twelve-year-old boy whose father has been killed in Vietnam.

Chapter 5, Section 66

- Billy tells the twelve-year-old about his adventures on Tralfamadore.
- Billy thinks the boy will be comforted to know that, according to the Tralfamadorians, his father is still alive in the moments before his death.
- The boy's mother tells his receptionist that Billy has gone crazy.
- Barbara comes to take Billy home.

Chapter 6, Section 1

- Billy wakes up early on the day he's going to be shipped to Dresden.
- In the hospital beds next to him, Edgar Derby and Paul Lazzaro are sleeping.
- Billy wakes up because he feels a sudden animal magnetism.
- This animal magnetism seems to be coming from behind Billy's bed.
- Billy finds its source: his bizarre, fur-collared little coat.
- The coat has two little lumps in the lining that seem to be the source of this animal magnetism.
- Something tells Billy to leave these lumps alone. As long as he does not attempt to figure out what the lumps are, they will bring him good luck.

Chapter 6, Section 2

- Billy wakes up in his prison hospital.
- The Englishmen are outside digging themselves a new latrine.
- Inside the hospital, the Blue Fairy Godmother stops by to check on Paul Lazzaro and his broken arm.
- Lazzaro says he'll have the Blue Fairy Godmother killed after the war.
- The Blue Fairy Godmother basically says, not if I kill you first.
- Lazzaro tells the Godmother, "Why don't you go fuck yourself?"; the Godmother answers,

hilariously: "Don't think I haven't tried" (6.2.9).

Chapter 6, Section 3

- Paul Lazzaro tells Billy and Edgar Derby that his favorite thing in the whole wide world is revenge.
- He tells a really awful story about tricking a dog that had bitten him into swallowing sharp metal hidden in a piece of steak. The dog died in agony.

Chapter 6, Section 4

- Later, when Dresden is destroyed, Lazzaro isn't not thrilled.
- He likes to take his enemies one by one, and he doesn't want to involve innocent bystanders.

Chapter 6, Section 5

- Edgar Derby asks Lazzaro if he plans to feed the Blue Fairy Godmother clock springs in a piece of steak.
- Lazzaro says no; he's going to have the Blue Fairy Godmother shot a couple of years after the end of the war, when he's not expecting it.

Chapter 6, Section 6

- Edgar Derby asks who else is on Lazzaro's vengeance list.
- Lazzaro tells Derby to make sure he doesn't make either Lazzaro or Lazzaro's friends mad.
- Lazzaro has had one friend in the war, and he's already dead: Roland Weary.
- He points to Billy in the next bed and says he promised Weary that he would have Billy shot after the war is over.
- Lazzaro advises Billy to enjoy life while he can.

Chapter 6, Section 7

- As a time traveler, Billy has seen his own death.
- He claims that he will die on February 13, 1976.
- By 1976, Billy claims, the U.S. will have been totally dismantled into twenty smaller countries so that it will not threaten world peace.
- The night of his death, Billy will speak to a stadium full of people on the subject of aliens and time.
- He will inform the crowd that he is about to be shot by Paul Lazzaro, but that it's OK, because death is not so bad.
- Billy will tell the police detail trying to protect him that it's time for him to be dead for a while, and then to live again.
- Suddenly, a bullet will smash through his forehead.
- Billy will experience death for a time. It is simply a violet light and a hum, with nobody else there.

Chapter 6, Section 8

- Billy travels back in time to an hour after Lazzaro's death threat.
- He, Lazzaro, and Edgar Derby are all supposed to get dressed and join the other American prisoners. They are supposed to elect a leader by secret ballot.

Chapter 6, Section 9

- Billy walks across the prison yard carrying his coat wrapped around his hands.
- Derby imagines himself writing letters home, telling his wife that he is alive and well.
- Lazzaro is thinking about the people he's going to have shot and the women he's going to have sex with, whether they want to or not.
- As they cross the prison yard, they see an Englishman marking a line between the American and English sections of the compound.

Chapter 6, Section 10

- The American prisoners are lying down in the theater.
- Someone yells at Billy to shut the door – was he born in a barn?!

Chapter 6, Section 11

- Billy shuts the door of the long shed behind him and approaches the stage where *Cinderella* was performed the night before.
- Neither Billy nor Edgar Derby nor Paul Lazzaro have blankets of their own, so they curl up on the stage with the blue curtains for covering.
- Billy sees the silver boots that had been part of Cinderella's costume sitting under her throne.
- He tries on the boots: they fit just right. Billy *is* Cinderella.

Chapter 6, Section 12

- The head English guy – the British colonel – lectures the Americans about hygiene.
- He then tries to keep their attention through a vote for leader, but half of the Americans are sleeping.

Chapter 6, Section 13

- The colonel warns the Americans that once you stop worrying about how you look, you'll just curl up and die.
- He's seen it happen before.

Chapter 6, Section 14

- The British colonel tells all the American prisoners about his hygiene regimen.
- Then he tells them that he envies the Americans for heading to Dresden, which, he hears, is a beautiful city.
- The British colonel wraps up by reassuring everyone that they don't have to worry about bombs in Dresden because it is of no significant military importance.

Chapter 6, Section 15

- Edgar Derby gets elected the head American.
- Derby thanks the British colonel for his advice and promises he and the other Americans will follow it.
- Paul Lazzaro tells him to get lost.

Chapter 6, Section 16

- The Americans begin to feel a bit better.
- They march out of the compound with Billy at the head of the parade. He's wearing the silver Cinderella boots, his fur-collared coat wrapped around his hands, and a piece of blue curtain tied around him like a toga.
- Edgar Derby once again imagines the letters he will write to his wife about Dresden and how it will never be bombed.
- They march to the same train station where they arrived.
- The Americans see the body of the dead hobo frozen beside the track.

Chapter 6, Section 17

- The trip to Dresden is actually really nice: the prisoners have been fed and they have lots of cigarettes with them.
- They pull in to Dresden, which is the most beautiful city many of them have ever seen.
- Billy Pilgrim thinks Dresden looks like a Sunday School illustration of Heaven.
- Someone behind him – the narrator – says that it looks like Oz.
- (Which it really does – check out these images.)

Chapter 6, Section 18

- By 1945, all of the other major cities in Germany have been bombed to the ground. Dresden is still totally intact.
- The three things Dresden produces are medicine, processed food, and cigarettes.
- It's five o'clock in the afternoon, and most of the people are coming home from work.

Chapter 6, Section 19

- The men guarding the American prisoners in Dresden are all kids and old guys sworn into the army the day before the Americans arrive.
- They are a little nervous to be meeting American troops straight from the front.
- When they arrive at the train station to see Billy Pilgrim (in his blue toga and silver boots), Paul Lazzaro (who is clearly nuts), and Edgar Derby (filled with puffed up notions of patriotism and wisdom), they immediately relax.
- These Americans are ridiculous, nothing to be afraid of.

Chapter 6, Section 20

- As Billy and the hundred other American prisoners walk out of the railway yard, Billy becomes a star.
- Lots of people are out on the Dresden sidewalks coming home from work, and they see Billy and the rest of the prisoners.
- Billy looks ridiculous, which brings a bit of fun into their day.
- Billy finds Dresden enchanting.
- At the same time, as a time traveler, he knows the city will burn to the ground in a month.
- Billy touches the two magnetic lumps in the lining of his jacket.

Chapter 6, Section 21

- The entire bunch of prisoners stops at a red traffic light.
- A German surgeon and war veteran stops and looks at Billy.
- He finds Billy offensive in his ridiculous clothes. He thinks Billy is making a mockery of the war.
- Billy has no idea that the German surgeon thinks Billy is being clownish and ridiculous.
- Billy pulls out the two lumps from the lining of his jacket. They are a two-carat diamond and a partial denture.
- Billy smiles at the surgeon as he holds the two things out to him.

Chapter 6, Section 22

- The prisoners arrive at a building that had once been a slaughterhouse.
- The slaughterhouse does not get much business now that most of the livestock in

Germany has been killed and eaten.

- The Americans are brought to a building that once held pigs waiting to be slaughtered. Now it has bunk beds, a water tap, and a latrine.
- This is *Schlachthof-fünf*: Slaughterhouse-Five.

Chapter 7, Section 1

- Twenty-five years later, Billy gets onto a plane with his father-in-law, Lionel Merble.
- They are heading to an optometry conference in Montreal.
- Billy knows that the plane is going to crash, but he doesn't want to make a fool of himself by saying so.
- Valencia is waving to Billy and her father from outside the plane.

Chapter 7, Section 2

- There is a barbershop quartet on board the plane.
- Lionel asks them to sing a couple of Polish songs he likes, which they do.
- Billy has seen a Polish man hanged: it was three days after he got to Dresden, and the man was being executed for having sex with a German woman.

Chapter 7, Section 3

- Billy zips back in time to 1944, to the forest in Luxembourg where Roland Weary is shaking him.

Chapter 7, Section 4

- The barbershop quartet is in the middle of an old Bing Crosby number when their plane whacks into the side of Sugarbush Mountain, in Vermont.
- Everyone is killed except Billy and the copilot.
- The people who first arrive on the scene are a couple of Austrian ski instructors from a nearby ski resort.
- Billy has fractured his skull, and thinks they are part of World War II.
- When they find Billy, he whispers his address to them: Schlachthof-fünf.

Slaughterhouse-Five.

Chapter 7, Section 5

- As Billy is being carried down the mountain, he sees lots of young people dressed in ski gear.
- He thinks this is all part of some new phase of World War II.

Chapter 7, Section 6

- Billy undergoes brain surgery and then sleeps for two days.
- He has many dreams, some of which are true.

Chapter 7, Section 7

- Billy dreams of his first evening in Slaughterhouse-Five.
- Billy and Edgar are being watched by a sixteen-year old guard named Werner Gluck.
- The whole city is blacked out for fear of bombing, so Billy doesn't get to see the city lights twinkling in the twilight.

Chapter 7, Section 8

- Werner Gluck was raised in Dresden.
- He has no idea where the slaughterhouse kitchen is, so he doesn't know where to take Billy and Edgar Derby.
- He and Billy are rather similar; in fact, they are distant cousins.
- Gluck leads them to a building he thinks has the kitchen, but boy is he wrong.
- Instead, the door leads to a communal shower where 30 German refugee girls are bathing.
- This is the first time Gluck and Billy have ever seen a naked girl. It's old hat to Edgar Derby.

Chapter 7, Section 9

- By the time they find the communal kitchen, pretty much everyone has left.
- There is only one woman, a war widow, waiting to give them food.
- She asks Gluck if he isn't a bit young to be in the army (which he is).
- She asks Edgar Derby if he isn't a bit old to be in the army (which he is).
- She doesn't know what Billy's supposed to be.

Chapter 7, Section 10

- Lying in bed in Vermont, Billy also dreams of Dresden the month before it is destroyed.
- One of Billy's jobs is to put jars of malt syrup (link: http://www.wisegeek.com/what-is-barley-malt-syrup.htm) into boxes at a local factory.
- The syrup is enriched with vitamins and minerals, and everyone who works there secretly eats it all day long.
- There are spoons stashed all over the factory for people to taste this syrup on the sly, even though it's against the rules to eat on the job.
- Billy finds a hidden spoon on his second day.
- His whole body celebrates at the taste of this malt syrup.

Chapter 7, Section 11

- Edgar Derby sees that Billy has taken a spoonful of syrup.
- He knocks on the window he is cleaning to get Billy's attention.
- Billy opens the window and pops a spoonful of syrup into Edgar Derby's mouth.
- Derby bursts into tears.
- Billy grabs the spoon and hides it when he hears someone coming.

Chapter 8, Section 1

- Two days before the Dresden bombing, Howard W. Campbell, Jr. (the fictional American Nazi who wrote the essay quoted in previous sections about the poor behavior of American prisoners of war) visits Slaughterhouse-Five.
- He wants to recruit American guys to fight in a new *German* military unit on the Russian front.

Chapter 8, Section 2

- Campbell is wearing a totally bizarre uniform of his own design, a weird mix of American and Nazi symbols (a ten-gallon hat and cowboy boots decorated with swastikas and stars).
- Billy has been eating syrup all day and he has terrible heartburn. He can barely see Campbell through the tears in his eyes.

Chapter 8, Section 3

- Campbell's audience is sleepy and uncomfortable.
- Campbell offers them more food if they will only join this Free American Corps.
- He says they'll have to fight the Communists sooner or later – they may as well do it with the Germans.

Chapter 8, Section 4

- Edgar Derby stands up and tells Campbell that he's a tool.
- He talks about American government, freedom, justice, and fair play for all.
- He then tells Campbell that the Americans and the Russians are going to work together to crush Nazism.
- The sound of an air raid siren sends the Americans into the slaughterhouse meat locker for shelter.
- Campbell stays with the German guards.

Chapter 8, Section 5

- The following night the Dresden firebombing will take place.
- As Billy sits snoozing in the meat locker, he travels forward to the argument with his daughter, Barbara, that started out this story.
- She tells him she wants to kill Kilgore Trout, the science fiction writer Billy likes.

Chapter 8, Section 6

- Kilgore Trout lives in Ilium, about two miles from Billy Pilgrim. He has never made any money off his novels, so he makes a living managing newspaper subscription sales in Ilium.
- Billy meets Trout in 1964 when Trout is bullying a group of newspaper boys to sell more subscriptions.
- Billy recognizes Trout's face (having seen it on lots of book covers), but he can't place him. He wonders if Trout was a prisoner of war in Dresden.

Chapter 8, Section 7

- Trout has written a book about a money tree with twenty-dollar bills for leaves.
- The tree attracts people to it. They kill each other around its roots and fertilize the tree.

Chapter 8, Section 8

- Billy parks his Cadillac and waits for Trout to stop yelling at his newsboys.
- When the meeting ends, there is one boy left behind who wants to quit.
- Trout asks the kid if he is a gutless wonder.
- *The Gutless Wonder* is a title of another of Trout's books. This book was published in 1932, but it predicts the use of burning jellied gasoline as a weapon dropped from airplanes.
- The person who drops this burning gas is a robot with bad breath. No one minds that he has killed lots of people, but they won't spend time with him until he clears up his bad breath.

Chapter 8, Section 9

- The kid quits anyway, even though Trout yells at him.
- Now Trout is forced to deliver his own newspapers, and he doesn't even have a bike.
- Billy approaches Trout and asks, "are you *Kilgore* Trout?" (8.9.6).
- Trout is shocked that Billy knows of him as a writer. He doesn't even think of himself that way.

Chapter 8, Section 10

- Billy helps Trout deliver his papers.
- Trout is still shocked to have met a fan. He tells Billy he's never even seen his books on sale or advertised.
- Trout has only ever gotten one piece of fan mail, from one Eliot Rosewater.
- Trout is surprised to find out that Rosewater was a captain in World War II and not a fourteen-year-old.

Chapter 8, Section 11

- Billy invites Trout to his eighteenth wedding anniversary party.
- Trout comes to the party and everyone likes him.
- He chats up Maggie White, a homemaker married to an optometrist.
- Billy listens while fiddling with something in his pocket: a box containing a ring for his wife.

Chapter 8, Section 12

- Trout is high on all of the unexpected attention he is getting at Billy's party.
- Maggie White asks Trout what his most famous book is.
- Trout makes something up about a funeral for a great French chef.

Chapter 8, Section 13

- Maggie asks if what Kilgore described *really happened.*
- Maggie is not bright, but she's really hot.
- Trout says of course it happened: he can't be guilty of false advertising – it's against the rules. (He's lying, of course.)
- Trout claims that he puts everything that happens to him into his books. And, he adds, he's not the only judge: there's also God, who will decide whether or not Maggie will burn in hell forever.
- Trout starts to laugh while Maggie looks terrified.

Chapter 8, Section 14

- An optometrist raises a toast to Billy and Valencia.
- There is a performance by the same barbershop quartet that sang to Billy and Lionel Merble on the fatal plane ride to Montreal.
- Billy suddenly feels upset by the song, "That Old Gang of Mine" (listen to it here!). Even though he has never had a gang, he misses them.

Chapter 8, Section 15

- Billy looks strange and several people around him notice that something is wrong.
- Valencia asks if he is OK.
- Billy says that he's fine, but he is really worried: he doesn't know why the song affected him so badly. He realizes that there is a secret inside of him that even he doesn't know.

Chapter 8, Section 16

- Billy starts to look a bit better, so people drift away. Only his wife and Trout remain.
- Trout guesses that Billy has seen through a *time window* into the past or the future.
- Billy says no and hands Valencia her gift.
- Valencia is excited and displays the ring for everyone to see.

Chapter 8, Section 17

- All the people at the party comment on what good jewelry Billy gives to Valencia.
- Maggie says Valencia already has the biggest diamond she has ever seen.
- The diamond is the one Billy finds in the lining of his coat during the war. He keeps the partial denture with his cufflinks in his dresser drawer.

Chapter 8, Section 18

- Billy seems normal, but Trout keeps following him, certain that something is going on.
- Trout tells Billy that he looked like he suddenly realized he was standing on thin air.

Chapter 8, Section 19

- The barbershop quartet starts singing again and Billy freaks out.
- He realizes that it's the four men singing in itself, not *what* they are singing, that is freaking him out.
- He rushes upstairs.

Chapter 8, Section 20

- Trout would have followed Billy upstairs but Billy told him not to.
- Billy goes into the bathroom and locks the door.
- His son Robert is sitting in the bathroom on the toilet in the dark, holding a pink electric guitar.
- Billy does not really know Robert yet – in fact, he is not sure if there is much *to* know.

Chapter 8, Section 21

- While the party is still going on downstairs, Billy lies down on his bed and turns on the Magic Fingers.

Chapter 8, Section 22

- Billy thinks about the barbershop quartet and why it worries him so much.
- He remembers (he does not travel in time, he remembers) the night Dresden was destroyed.
- He and the Americans and four of their guards are sheltering in the meat locker, which is deep, cool, and safe.
- Outside people are being killed all around them: the other guards and their families, the refugee girls, everyone in the neighborhood.
- It isn't safe for them to leave their shelter until noon the next day.
- When they come out, they see that the sky is black with smoke and the stones themselves are still hot.

Chapter 8, Section 23

- The four guards look around with their mouths open in shock. They remind Billy of a silent film of a barbershop quartet.
- It is as though they are singing "That Old Gang of Mine": "So long forever . . . old fellows and pals" (8.23.2).

Chapter 8, Section 24

- One night, when she is six months pregnant and living in the middle of the Tralfamadorian zoo, Montana asks Billy to tell her a story.
- Billy tells her that Dresden, Germany, was destroyed on February 13, 1945.
- He tells her about the guards who looked like a barbershop quartet and the remains of people caught in the firestorm all over the city.
- He tells her the ruins of the city looked like the moon.

Chapter 8, Section 25

- The guards form the prisoners into groups of four and march them over to the pig shelter where they used to live.
- The shelter is destroyed, and everyone realizes they have no food and water. They have to search for it.

Chapter 8, Section 26

- As the Americans walk through the remains of the city, they realize that the ground is not as stable as it looks. They keep slipping and falling into the ruins.
- They say nothing as they walk: there is nothing appropriate to say.

Chapter 8, Section 27

- American fighter planes drop below the smoke to shoot anything moving in the ruins.
- They shoot at Billy and the American prisoners but no one is killed.
- They shoot at another group of moving people, and some of them are hit.

Chapter 8, Section 28

- By nightfall, the guards and the Americans come upon a totally bizarre sight: an inn open for business.
- There are empty beds and tables and chairs enough for everyone.
- The inn is being run by a blind man, his sighted wife, and their two young daughters.
- The family knows that Dresden is gone, that it has been burned to the ground, but they still opened their inn for the day.
- The four guards and hundred American prisoners are their first guests.
- The guards tell the innkeeper that no one else is coming, that they haven't seen anyone alive all day.

Chapter 8, Section 29

- The innkeeper says that the Americans can sleep in his stable that night, and he feeds them.
- He comes in to wish them a good night: "Good night, Americans. . . . Sleep well" (8.29.2).

Chapter 9, Section 1

- Valencia hears about Billy's plane crash on Sugarbush Mountain, Vermont.
- The doctors tell her that Billy's head injury means that he could die or be a vegetable.
- As she drives to the hospital, Valencia gets so upset that she misses the turnoff on the highway, hits the breaks, and gets rear-ended by a Mercedes.
- No one is seriously hurt, but Valencia's Cadillac's rear fender is smashed up and her exhaust pipe falls off.
- Valencia can still drive the car, so she puts it in gear and continues her drive to the hospital.
- Driving without an exhaust pipe turns out to have been a bad idea, though. By the time she gets to the hospital, Valencia has been exposed to too much carbon monoxide.
- She winds up dying from carbon monoxide poisoning an hour after getting to the hospital.

Chapter 9, Section 2

- Meanwhile, Billy is still unconscious.
- Billy is sharing a room with a (fictional) Harvard history professor named Bertram Copeland Rumfoord.
- Rumfoord is in the hospital with a broken leg. He injured himself while skiing on his honeymoon with his fifth (and much younger) wife, Lily.

Chapter 9, Section 3

- At the same moment that Valencia is being pronounced dead, Lily comes into Rumfoord's hospital room with a bunch of books Rumfoord wants for his research on the history of the U.S. Air Corps.
- The books are all about battles of World War II.

Chapter 9, Section 4

- Billy is muttering in his sleep, reliving his memories of the War.
- Lily whispers to Rumfoord that Billy *scares* her.
- Rumfoord replies that he finds Billy *boring*: all he does in his sleep is surrender and apologize and ask to be left alone.
- Rumfoord is a hyper-masculine, super-rich, all-around successful guy. He finds Billy utterly pathetic.
- Rumfoord then asks Lily if she has read President Harry Truman's announcement of the atomic bombing of Hiroshima in August 1945.
- Lily sits down and pretends to read it.
- The novel then quotes from Truman's announcement, which gives the reasons why Truman feels the atomic bomb is both necessary and scientifically remarkable.

Chapter 9, Section 5

- Among the books Lily brings Rumfoord is *The Destruction of Dresden*, by David Irving.
- In it, Ira C. Eakerz, an Air Force General, makes a case for the necessity of firebombing Dresden.
- British Air Marshal Sir Robert Saundby writes that it was not necessary, but that it happened, as these things sometimes do in wartime. What is immoral is war itself.

- Billy mutters about Cody, Wyoming, and Wild Bob in his sleep.
- Lily shudders.

Chapter 9, Section 6

- Later that day, Barbara Pilgrim comes to visit Billy in the hospital.
- She has been given some tranquilizers to help keep her functional in the wake of her father's injury and her mother's death.
- She looks glassy-eyed, like Edgar Derby before the firing squad shot him.
- Robert Pilgrim is flying back from Vietnam.
- Barbara speaks to Billy, but he can't hear her: he is in 1958, examining the vision of a boy with Down's syndrome.

Chapter 9, Section 7

- Billy travels in time to when he is sixteen years old and sitting in a doctor's waiting room.
- Another man is waiting to see the doctor.
- The man is elderly and he is having terrible problems with gas. He keeps farting loudly and apologizing.
- The man exclaims that getting old *sucks*.

Chapter 9, Section 8

- Billy opens his eyes in the hospital in Vermont, where he sees his son Robert.
- Robert is all dressed up in his Green Beret uniform and he looks like "a leader of men" (9.8.2).
- Robert was a wild teenager, but the army has straightened him out.
- Billy closes his eyes again.

Chapter 9, Section 9

- Billy misses Valencia's funeral because he is still in the hospital.
- He has been so listless in response to her death and Robert's return that the doctors think he might be a vegetable.

* He's only listless on the outside, though; on the inside, Billy is preparing lectures on the true nature of time.

Chapter 9, Section 10

* Rumfoord thinks Billy is brain dead and tells Lily that the hospital should just let him die.
* Lily doesn't know what to think; she's not very bright.
* Rumfoord talks to Lily about his problems with the bombing of Dresden.
* He wants to write a short, readable version of the *Official History of the Army Air Force in World War II*.
* That lengthy history has very little information about Dresden.
* Rumfoord wants to know why. The bombing was such a roaring success! Why don't more Americans know about it?

Chapter 9, Section 11

* Rumfoord decides that he has to include something about Dresden in his book.
* Why has it been kept secret for so long?, Lily asks.
* Because the Air Force was worried about bleeding hearts who might think it was the wrong thing to do, answers Rumfoord.
* Billy then speaks up to tell Rumfoord and Lily that he was there.

Chapter 9, Section 12

* Rumfoord cannot believe Billy is speaking – he was sure he was a vegetable.
* He doesn't understand him at first and needs to have Billy's words explained to him by Lily.

Chapter 9, Section 13

* Rumfoord decides Billy has echolalia, a mental illness that makes people repeat what they hear others around them saying.
* Rumfoord is wrong, but he wants Billy to have this illness because he finds him inconvenient.

Chapter 9, Section 14

- Rumfoord keeps telling all the doctors and nurses that Billy has echolalia.
- All the doctors and nurses think Rumfoord is a jerk, and no one believes him.

Chapter 9, Section 15

- Billy lies in bed trying to convince Rumfoord that he's telling the truth.
- He waits for a long time to say that he was at Dresden, just to prove to Rumfoord that he is not echoing.
- Rumfoord still doesn't believe him.
- Billy tells him that they don't have to talk about it, but he just wants Rumfoord to know that he was there.

Chapter 9, Section 16

- Billy closes his eyes and travels to May 1945, two days after the end of World War II in Europe (the war doesn't end in the Pacific theater until August 1945).
- He and five other American prisoners are traveling back to their Dresden slaughterhouse for souvenirs of war.
- Billy is warm and happy: he and the prisoners had managed to take food, wine, a stamp collection, a camera, a stuffed owl, and a clock from an abandoned house.
- The owners had left their house because they had heard that the Russians were coming, and that they were doing terrible things to people they found.

Chapter 9, Section 17

- Billy stays in the wagon sunning himself while the others go looking for souvenirs inside the slaughterhouse.
- This afternoon nap is one of his happiest memories.

Chapter 9, Section 18

- While he is napping, Billy is armed for the first time since basic training.
- He has scavenged a World War I–era pistol and a Luftwaffe (German air force) sword from the ruins of the city.

Chapter 9, Section 19

- Billy wakes up to see a middle-aged German couple speaking softly to the horses who have been drawing his wagon.
- The animals are absolutely miserable: their hooves have been broken by the ruins of the city and they are insane with thirst. Every step has been agony for them.

Chapter 9, Section 20

- The couple is not afraid of Billy, who continues to look ridiculous in his toga and silver shoes.
- They are both obstetricians who delivered babies until the hospitals burned down. They are a handsome couple, and they speak nine languages between them.
- Billy asks them in English what they want, and they immediately answer.
- They yell at Billy for treating the horses so badly and make him come look at the state they're in.
- Billy cries for the first and last time during the War.

Chapter 9, Section 21

- After the war, Billy will cry suddenly, out of the blue. But he never makes loud sobbing noises.
- This is why the narrator has chosen "Away in a Manger" as the epigraph for the novel: like the little Jesus in the Christmas carol, "No crying [Billy] makes" (9.21.2).
- Billy travels in time to his hospital bed in Vermont, where Rumfoord has finally decided that, yes, Billy *was* at Dresden.
- He asks Billy what it was like, and Billy tells Rumfoord about the horses and the moonscape of the ruined city.
- The story ends like this: Billy and the doctors unharness the horses, but they don't go anywhere because their feet hurt too much.

- Just then, the Russians come in and arrest everyone.
- Two days after that, Billy gets turned over to the American authorities, who send him home.
- A minor observation: the narrator specifies that Billy gets sent home on a ship named after American women's rights activist Lucretia A. Mott. But Lucretia Mott's middle name was Coffin, so it would be Lucretia C. Mott. Accident? Or deliberate substitution because Vonnegut didn't want to talk about Coffins in this scene. Who can say?

Chapter 9, Section 22

- Rumfoord tells Billy that the bombing of Dresden *had* to happen, but admits that it must have sucked to be there.
- Rumfoord acknowledges that Billy probably has mixed feelings about the bombing because he was an eyewitness.
- Billy says it's all right because he has learned on Tralfamadore that everyone has to do exactly what he does.

Chapter 9, Section 23

- Barbara brings Billy home later in the day and puts him to bed.
- Billy manages to sneak out of the house and head to New York City, where he wants to tell the world about Tralfamadore.

Chapter 9, Section 24

- Billy checks into the Royalton Hotel in midtown Manhattan.
- He looks down from his top floor room at all of the people walking around on the streets below.
- He turns on the TV.

Chapter 9, Section 25

- Billy walks over to Times Square and looks in the window of a pornographic bookstore.
- There's lots of raunchy stuff in there, but there are also four totally neglected novels by

Kilgore Trout.

Chapter 9, Section 26

- Billy goes in to the bookstore and sees both pornographic pictures and movies.
- The pictures are very Tralfamadorian because you can take them home and look at them and they will always be exactly the same.
- But what Billy really wants are the Kilgore Trout novels in the window.
- He doesn't recognize the titles, but when he opens one, he realizes he has read it after all.
- It's about a man and a woman from Earth who are kidnapped by aliens and put in a zoo.

Chapter 9, Section 27

- In Trout's novel, the aliens give the two Earthlings a fake stock market ticker.
- They tell the Earthlings that this is connected to the stock markets back on Earth, and that they now have a million dollars in investments in the market.
- This is all a lie: the aliens just want to make the Earthlings perform for them in their zoo.
- But the humans think they are making a ton of money back on Earth.
- They also try religion: when they have a bad week on the market, they give prayer a whirl.
- It seems to work, too: their fake stocks go up after they pray.

Chapter 9, Section 28

- Another Trout novel is about a man who builds a time machine to go back and visit Jesus.
- He appears when Jesus is twelve years old and working with his dad as a carpenter.
- A couple of Roman soldiers stop by with a plan for an execution device they want Jesus and his dad to build for them.
- They build the device according to the Romans' design.
- A rabble-rouser is executed using the device.

Chapter 9, Section 29

- The porn shop is run by five apparently identical short, bald guys.
- These five guys and Billy Pilgrim are the only ones in the store without an erection.

- A clerk tells Billy these Kilgore Trout novels are window dressing – what Billy really wants is in the back.
- Billy goes toward the back of the store, but he keeps reading the Trout novel.
- The hero of the novel travels back in time because he wants to know if Jesus really died on the cross or if he was taken down while he was still alive.
- The time traveler gets to Jesus' cross just when he is about to be taken down. He grabs a ladder and climbs up to check Jesus' heartbeat with a stethoscope.
- Jesus' heart is not beating. He is absolutely dead.
- The time traveler also measures how tall Jesus is. He is five foot three.

Chapter 9, Section 30

- A clerk asks Billy if he is going to buy the book or what.
- He thinks Billy is reading something from the rack behind him on the history of oral sex.
- When he sees that Billy is reading a Kilgore Trout novel, he tells all the other clerks to come and check out this pervert.
- The cash register is next to a stack of old magazines, one of which has the headline: "What really became of Montana Wildhack?" (9.30.2).

Chapter 9, Section 31

- Billy reads the magazine.
- Of course, he knows that Montana Wildhack is back on Tralfamadore raising their child.
- The magazine, however, claims that she has drowned in San Pedro Bay.
- The magazine ran this article because they wanted to use photographs from porn flicks that Montana made when she was a teenager.
- Seeing his interest, the clerks send Billy back to the rear of the shop, where he can watch a film with Montana Wildhack in it.
- He goes, but he doesn't really watch – instead, a clerk leads him over to "some really hot stuff they keep under the counter" (9.31.4): a picture of a woman trying to have sex with a Shetland pony between two Greek columns. (Just like Roland Weary's picture in Chapter 2, Section 22.)

Chapter 9, Section 32

- Billy fails to make it onto TV in New York, but he does get on a radio talk show.

- He claims he is from the *Ilium Gazette*. The people at the radio show think he is a literary critic there to talk about the state of the novel.
- Billy remembers Wild Bob, the American colonel who died in front of Billy on the train to the POW compound in Germany.

Chapter 9, Section 33

- The debate at the radio show is over whether the novel is dead. (Believe it or not, this has been a discussion between public intellectuals and writers for most of the twentieth century.)
- Billy then gets to speak, and he tells the world about the Tralfamadorians and Montana Wildhack and all the rest of it.
- He's booted out of the radio station during a commercial break.
- He goes back to his hotel room and falls asleep with the Magic Fingers working.
- He wakes up on Tralfamadore with Montana Wildhack, who is breast-feeding their baby.
- Billy tells Montana that he has been walking around Times Square and that he watched part of a porno she was in.
- Montana says OK. She says she has heard about what a clown Billy was during the war.
- There is a silver locket hanging between Montana's breasts that holds a picture of her mother. Engraved on it are the words, "God grant me the serenity to accept the things I cannot change, courage to change the things I can, and wisdom always to tell the difference" (9.33.21).
- (Does this ring a bell? You might remember that Billy's optometry office has the same saying framed on the wall in Chapter 3, Section 13.)

Chapter 10, Section 1

- The narrator tells us that Robert Kennedy died the night before, that Martin Luther King, Jr. died a month ago, and that every night, he sees the body count coming out of Vietnam.
- The narrator's father was a nice guy who collected guns, which he left to the narrator when he died. They rust.

Chapter 10, Section 2

- Billy tells us that Tralfamadorians aren't that interested in Jesus.
- The Earthling they really like is Charles Darwin, who has taught us that those who die are

meant to in order to improve the species.

Chapter 10, Section 3

- Trout uses this idea in a novel called *The Big Board*, in which the aliens ask the hero about Darwin and golf.

Chapter 10, Section 4

- The narrator says that he's not thrilled at the Tralfamadorian idea that we all live forever.
- Still, if we have to visit moments in our lives forever, he is glad that so many of his moments are nice.
- One of the narrator's nicest recent moments is his trip to Dresden with his old war buddy, Bernard V. O'Hare.
- The narrator looks down from his Hungarian Airlines plane on East Germany, which is all lit up.
- The narrator imagines dropping bombs on the cities and towns below him.

Chapter 10, Section 5

- The narrator and O'Hare never expected to make any money, and yet they have.
- The narrator says to O'Hare: "If you're ever in Cody, Wyoming . . . just ask for Wild Bob" (10.5.2).

Chapter 10, Section 6

- O'Hare is reading a book of world facts about altitudes of major mountains and distances between cities and whatnot.
- He shows the narrator a little blurb in the book that predicts there will be seven billion people on the planet by the year 2000.
- All of those people will want dignity, comments the narrator.

Chapter 10, Section 7

- Billy is back in 1945, two days after the bombing of Dresden, marching into the ruins with his guards.
- The narrator and Bernard O'Hare are also both there.
- They are being given pickaxes and shovels so they can get to work digging through Dresden.

Chapter 10, Section 8

- There are barricades leading to the ruins of Dresden.
- No German civilians are being allowed in.

Chapter 10, Section 9

- Prisoners of war from all over Germany are being forced to dig through the ruins of Dresden looking for bodies.
- Billy is paired with a Maori soldier who had been captured at the Siege of Tobruk.
- They break through a thin layer of rocks to find the first of many groups of bodies huddled together under the rubble.

Chapter 10, Section 10

- The corpses don't smell bad at first, but they slowly start to rot. The smell is like roses and mustard gas.
- The Maori whom Billy had been working with cannot handle the smell and winds up dying from dry heaves.
- To prevent this kind of thing from happening again, the soldiers stop bringing the bodies out of their holes. They start using flamethrowers to destroy them on the spot.
- In the ruins, Edgar Derby is caught stealing a teapot from the rubble. He is arrested, tried for looting, and shot.
- Billy and the other American prisoners wind up locked up in a stable on the outskirts of the city.
- Suddenly one day, the door is opened: the war in Europe is over.
- Billy and his fellow prisoners go outside and find that it is spring. The leaves are green and there is no one around.

- The birds are speaking to each other.
- One says to Billy Pilgrim: "Poo-tee-weet?" (10.10.11).

Themes

Theme of Fate and Free Will

In *Slaughterhouse-Five*, the primary upshot of what Billy Pilgrim learns from the plunger-shaped aliens is: if we cannot change anything about time, there is no such thing as free will. After all, free will means the ability to alter your own future. In fact, the Tralfamadorians tell Billy that the whole idea of free will seems to be unique to Earthlings. Everyone else in the universe knows better. Billy uses this knowledge to comfort himself about the realities of aging, death, and pain. Even if human beings have to suffer, at least there is nothing to be done about it.

We don't think Billy's resignation is necessarily a good thing. Sure, it makes him feel better. But it also lets him off the hook: if you can't improve the world, why bother? The book comments that it is in moments of struggle that otherwise one-dimensional figures become real characters. One example is Edgar Derby's confrontation with Howard W. Campbell, Jr., when the narrator tells us that, "There are almost no characters in this story . . . But old Derby was a character now" (8.4.1). What makes Derby a character is his willingness to try to do something he thinks is right – and yeah, he may not achieve anything, but at least he tries.

Questions About Fate and Free Will

1. What connections does the novel seem to draw between having "character" and having free will? Who are the real characters in the novel, if any?
2. Why is the Tralfamadorian idea of time incompatible with free will?
3. Does Billy Pilgrim exercise his own will at any point in the novel? If so, when?

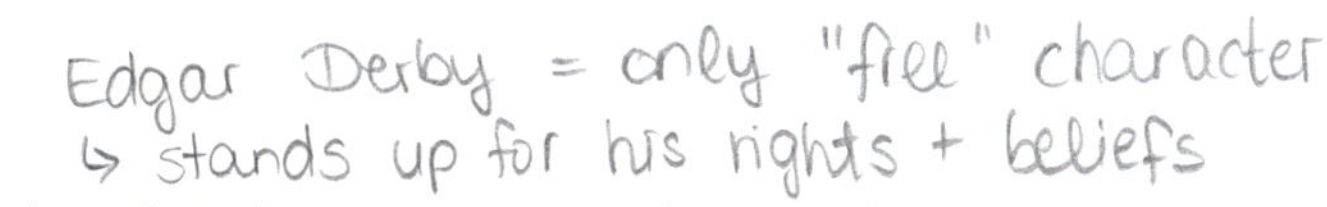

Edgar Derby = only "free" character
↳ stands up for his rights + beliefs

Chew on Fate and Free Will

Edgar Derby only becomes a character when he chooses to stand up against American Nazi Howard W. Campbell, Jr. It's this decision to stand up for what he believes in that distinguishes Derby from other people in the novel.

When Billy chooses to tell the world about Tralfamadore, it's the first and last truly independent decision he makes. However, his effort to make his own choices gets undercut by his daughter and the general public, who all think Billy is crazy. Everyone in the novel operates under so many social and familial constraints on their freedom that the attempt to make one's own

choices appears insane.

Theme of Warfare

Slaughterhouse-Five is about a very particular experience of war. This book isn't about officers or heroes. It's about privates, most of whom don't want to be – and shouldn't be – on the battlefield. And it's about prisoners of war, men who have been deprived of any kind of control over where they go and what they do. There is nothing romantic about war in *Slaughterhouse-Five*. In fact, the villains of the novel are the ones who continue to romanticize violence and killing, men like Bertram Copeland Rumfoord and even foolish Roland Weary.

Questions About Warfare

1. How does the narrator counteract potential justifications for the bombing of Dresden within *Slaughterhouse-Five*? How does he represent characters who approve of this firebombing?
2. Which characters in the book glorify war? How does the narrator represent these characters? What kind of commentary might *Slaughterhouse-Five* be making on those who glorify war?
3. Why does *Slaughterhouse-Five* avoid any direct representations of the battlefield? Why should a book about World War II focus so much on people who are *not* fighting?
4. Vonnegut refers to the Vietnam War and the assassinations of Robert Kennedy and Martin Luther King, Jr. While the content of the novel clearly focuses on World War II, how is *Slaughterhouse-Five* also a book about America in the 1960s?

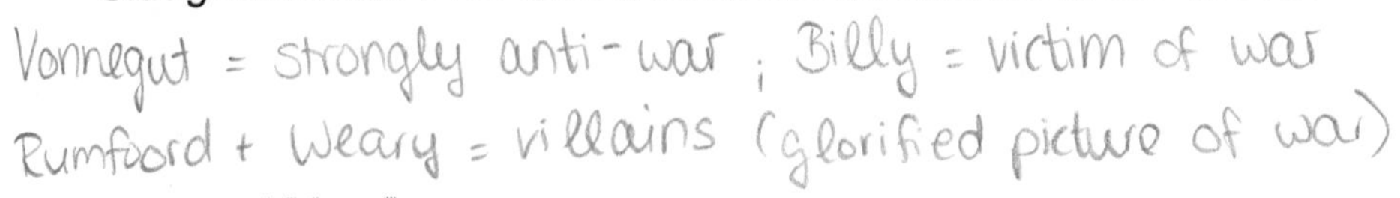

Vonnegut = strongly anti-war ; Billy = victim of war
Rumfoord + Weary = villains (glorified picture of war)

Chew on Warfare

By giving villainous characters like Roland Weary and Bertram Copeland Rumfoord a love of war (or the idea of war, at least), Vonnegut conveys his strongly anti-war sentiments to the reader.

By avoiding representations of the battlefield and focusing instead on prisoners of war, Vonnegut draws the reader's attention not to war itself, but to the suffering it causes.

Theme of Time

Billy Pilgrim and the narrator of *Slaughterhouse-Five* both spend a fair amount of their time reliving their experiences in World War II. The narrator recalls the war through personal memory, historical research, and travel with his war buddy to Dresden, the site of his most painful experiences. Billy travels to the past a little more literally: he never knows when he's going to be sent from his optometry practice or his home right back to the POW compound or the slaughterhouse in Dresden where he spent part of the war. Billy has so little control over his own life that he doesn't even know *when* he will be, let alone where, from one moment to the

next. His only cure is to take refuge in the beliefs of the Tralfamadorians: that death, free will, and time itself are all illusions.

Questions About Time

1. How does the Tralfamadorian idea of time appear to affect the very structure of *Slaughterhouse-Five*?
2. Why does the narrator distinguish between Billy's *memories* of the barbershop quartet in Chapter 8, Section 14, and Billy's time travel? Can Billy remember things without moving through time?
3. The one moment in the book when Billy flashes forward to a time beyond Tralfamadore is his vision of his own death in Chapter 6, Section 7. Is this scene described any differently from his usual time travel *back* to the various points of life he has already lived? Are there any indications in the text that we are not supposed to take Billy's predictions for 1976 seriously?

Chew on Time

Slaughterhouse-Five uses the Tralfamadorian idea of time as an organizing principle to blur the lines between the novel's form and content.

Billy's death scene, in which he is surrounded by adoring crowds and goes bravely to his death at the hands of Paul Lazzaro, reads like a fantasy. On the other hand, his flashbacks to his early history show how fundamentally powerless he is and has always been.

Theme of Suffering

From Billy's excessively realistic crucified Christ (Chapter 2, Section 19) to the horses with shattered hooves in the rubble of Dresden (Chapter 9, Section 19), much of the suffering in *Slaughterhouse-Five* explicitly targets innocents. Billy is a foolish, inexperienced boy who is sent to the front lines of a war he does not understand. The injustice of suffering – that it should strike the people who seem least equipped to understand or deal with it – is yet another reason Billy turns to science fiction and Tralfamadore to make himself a new reality. His current, agonizing reality no longer makes any sense to Billy, so he needs another one.

Questions About Suffering

1. Why does Vonnegut spend time on the suffering of animals (the horses in Chapter 9, Section 19 and the frightened German shepherd in Chapter 3, Section 1)?
2. How do characters like Roland Weary and Paul Lazzaro add to the suffering of their comrades? Can we deduce anything about human nature from their behavior as POWs?
3. How does Vonnegut seem to link Christianity with suffering? Why can't Billy find comfort

for his suffering in the Christian church?

Chew on Suffering

By showing the thoughtless cruelty to animals of even well-meaning characters like Billy, Vonnegut demonstrates that suffering is often an unintended side-effect of war.

Billy does not use the Christian faith as a comfort for his postwar stress and misery because he associates the church with the painful sacrifice of an innocent man, of which Billy has already seen plenty.

Theme of Morality and Ethics

The Tralfamadorians are pretty clear that their novels hold no moral lessons for readers. After all, what would be the point of a moral lesson when you can't do anything to change the future? *Slaughterhouse-Five*, with its stars and tiny sections, seems to be imitating a Tralfamadorian novel. So it makes sense that the narrator doesn't spend much time preaching about right or wrong: that's not the point of this book.

If the book were really trying to deliver a moral message, the narrator's emphasis on the suffering of the Germans in Dresden might have to be balanced out by a much longer meditation on the Nazis' concentration camps. What Vonnegut seems to be asking his readers to do instead is to think about how much human suffering the war brought for both sides. Some of the most evil characters in the book – Bertram Copeland Rumfoord and Paul Lazzaro – are the ones who think they are absolutely right. This kind of righteous self-assurance is what leads to war in the first place.

Questions About Morality and Ethics

1. Vonnegut may not give us clear-cut moral lessons (us versus them, Americans versus Germans), but he does have a strongly ethical anti-war message. How does Vonnegut present this anti-war message through Billy Pilgrim's plot in the novel?
2. Why do the Tralfamadorians *not* believe in morality? What do they have instead?
3. Do we ever see any moments in the novel when Billy could intervene morally and doesn't? Why not?

Chew on Morality and Ethics

The narrator tells his sons in Chapter 1 that they are not to participate in massacres, but Billy Pilgrim willingly sends his son Robert off to Vietnam, presumably to kill people. This difference between the narrator's and Billy's choices exposes a fundamental difference between the two

men's characters: Billy is resigned to war, while the narrator is trying to prevent fighting.

By focusing on the suffering of individual human beings, such as the German refugee girls killed in the Dresden firebombing, Vonnegut shifts attention about the morality of war away from big questions of national politics toward smaller, less justifiable instances of personal pain.

Theme of Foolishness and Folly

Because *Slaughterhouse-Five* is an anti-war book, Vonnegut isn't presenting us with any heroes. And to counteract the impression that any of the men in the novel have the self-determination or free will to make heroic choices, *Slaughterhouse-Five* relies a lot on absurdity. Billy Pilgrim is described repeatedly as clownish; he looks so ridiculous that a German surgeon on the streets of Dresden criticizes him for making a mockery of war. Paul Lazzaro and Roland Weary are both so self-absorbed that they don't even seem to notice that they are on a battlefield half the time. And even poor Edgar Derby, who is so idealistic and committed, can be reduced to tears by the unexpected taste of syrup in his mouth by the end of the war.

Still, the real foolishness in the book is not at the individual level. We can't help but think there must be something wrong with a system that would send poor, innocent Billy Pilgrim to war.

Questions About Foolishness and Folly

1. Why is Billy Pilgrim, the main character of *Slaughterhouse-Five*, repeatedly represented as a clown? How does this differ from traditional representations of men in wartime?
2. We know that Billy Pilgrim, Roland Weary, and Paul Lazzaro are all fools, but what about Edgar Derby? How does Vonnegut represent his idealism and faith in truth and justice?
3. There is enough folly to go around among the individual characters of *Slaughterhouse-Five* , but how does Vonnegut hint at the foolishness of the men in command of the war?

Chew on Foolishness and Folly

Edgar Derby's belief in justice may be foolish, but the narrator also expresses sympathy for his efforts to resist a system he believes is wrong

Billy Pilgrim continues to appear clownish throughout his entire wartime experience because the narrator explicitly wants to describe World War II as a Children's Crusade. Billy is the ultimate foolish innocent sent into a battle he does not understand.

Theme of Freedom and Confinement

Obviously, *Slaughterhouse-Five* is a book about prisoners of war, and it doesn't get much more confined than that. But even more, it's a book about the many, many ways people get trapped:

by the army, by family, and by their own beliefs in God or glory. It isn't only the Germans or the U.S. Army who take away Billy's choices. He also finds himself caving in to the expectations of his mother, his optometry office, and even his own daughter. Billy sees very little real freedom in his life, which is perhaps why he is so eager to accept that there is no such thing as free will.

Questions About Freedom and Confinement

1. What comparisons does Vonnegut suggest between the Germans who took Billy captive and the Tralfamadorians? What significance might these comparisons have?
2. Billy is (obviously) a prisoner of war, but what else might we say he is a prisoner of? What other kinds of less-tangible confinement do he and the other characters suffer?
3. In what ways does Billy remain a prisoner of the Germans even after he returns home at the end of the war?

Chew on Freedom and Confinement

The Germans and the Tralfamadorians both take away Billy's freedom, but the Tralfamadorians go a step further by giving him the tools he needs to accept his confinement.

Even after Billy is freed from German captivity, he remains mentally a prisoner of his war experiences – until he can replace these memories with life on Tralfamadore.

Theme of Men and Masculinity

In the first chapter of *Slaughterhouse-Five*, the narrator promises Mary O'Hare that he will write a novel about World War II that will *not* attract the attention of manly men like John Wayne or Frank Sinatra. One way in which Vonnegut certainly succeeds in making war seem utterly unappealing (besides, you know, the death and pain and misery) is by emphasizing the hunger and illness of the soldiers fighting it. Paul Lazzaro's stomach is shrunken with hunger, Edgar Derby weeps at the taste of syrup, and all the American POWs spend their first night in the British compound with explosive diarrhea. The book really foregrounds the unattractive, absurd realities of male bodies under stress. The only soldiers with big muscles and washboard abs are the English officers, who have been prisoners for the whole war, and who barely fight.

Questions About Men and Masculinity

1. Who are the stereotypical "real men" in this novel? Why are they not fighting on the front lines? What kind of commentary might Vonnegut be giving about the realities of war?
2. As with everything Tralfamadorian, the aliens' idea of gender really differs from Earth's binary two-gender system. What might be the purpose of these multiple genders?
3. How do American male bodies get depicted in *Slaughterhouse-Five*? Why?

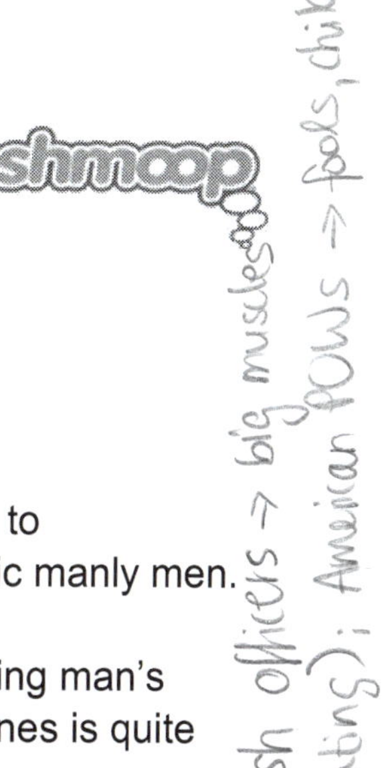

shmoop
British officers → big muscles; American POWs → fools, children (fighting)

Chew on Men and Masculinity

Kurt Vonnegut depicts the bodies of the American POWs as weak and poorly fed to demonstrate that this is a war being fought by fools and children rather than heroic manly men.

The contrast between British and American POWs shows that maintaining a fighting man's body in captivity is one thing, but staying healthy, warm, and strong on the front lines is quite another.

Theme of Literature and Writing

As we discussed in "Genre," *Slaughterhouse-Five* really draws attention to the fact that it's a book, being written by an author. This is part of what makes it a "postmodern" novel (see "Genre" for more on this). With a more traditional novel, you read it as though it's a direct representation of something that *really* happens (even though you know it's fiction). In other words, you forget that you're reading a novel. But readers of *Slaughterhouse-Five* can never fall into this illusion. The narrator introduces the book and pops up throughout its "fictional" sections to remind us that "Billy Pilgrim" is a product of his imagination. At the same time, the blurring between the narrator's life and Billy Pilgrim's experiences challenge our ideas of what is fiction and what is truth.

Questions About Literature and Writing

1. We know the narrator opens and ends *Slaughterhouse-Five*, but where else in the book does he directly address the reader? Why?
2. What value does *Slaughterhouse-Five* assign to science fiction as a genre? How does the book draw on science fiction conventions to make its own points about fate and free will?
3. How do Tralfamadorian novels differ from Earth novels? How does *Slaughterhouse-Five* mimic a Tralfamadorian novel?

Chew on Literature and Writing *

The narrator appears occasionally in the "Billy Pilgrim" portions of the novel to remind us that, while the events Billy encounters in Germany may seem farfetched or unfamiliar, they are based on the narrator's lived experience.

Vonnegut uses the fictional structure of the Tralfamadorian novel to structure *Slaughterhouse-Five*. This emphasizes that both the narrator's introduction to the novel and Billy Pilgrim's portion of the story arise from the same place: Vonnegut himself.

* other sources:
bible, accounts on Dresden, announcement of Truman, Kilgore Trout's novels, Goethe, ...

Quotes

Fate and Free Will Quotes

So it goes.
(1.1.3, 1.21.2, 1.21.5, 2.2.1, 2.4.2, 2.7.3, 2.12.4, 2.16.2, 2.17.5, 2.19.16, 2.23.4, 2.27.2, 3.16.2, 3.22.1, 3.23.2, 4.3.1, 4.11.3-4, 4.14.2, 4.16.1, 4.16.4, 4.19.1, 5.5.2, 5.7.2, 5.8.2, 5.10.1, 5.10.3, 5.14.5, 5.20.8, 5.23.1, 5.24.12, 5.24.17, 5.27.12, 5.31.5, 5.38.1. 5.43.4, 5.55.10, 5.65.2, 6.5.6, 6.6.4, 6.9.3, 6.13.1, 6.16.4, 6.21.1 7.2.4, 7.4.1, 7.7.1, 7.9.1, 8.7.2, 8.12.7, 8.24.3, 8.27.1, 9.1.6, 9.5.9, 9.6.2, 9.19.1, 9.24.4, 9.28.4, 9.29.8, 9.32.1, 10.1.1-3, 10.10.2, 10.10.4, 10.10.7)

Thought: As you can see from the page citations on this one, "So it goes" is pretty much *the* signature stock phrase of the novel. It expresses a general sense of resignation to the way things are. Your champagne goes flat? So it goes. Somebody dies? So it goes. This is a Tralfamadorian motto, Billy Pilgrim explains, and he seems to embrace it. But we think the fact that the narrator has decided to write an anti-war book suggests that he does not find "so it goes" sufficient to explain all of the needless violence he has seen.

Billy first came unstuck while World War II was in progress. Billy was a chaplain's assistant in the war. A chaplain's assistant is customarily a figure of fun in the American Army. Billy was no exception. He was powerless to harm the enemy or to help his friends. In fact, he had no friends. He was a valet to a preacher, expected no promotions or medals, bore no arms, and had a meek faith in a loving Jesus which most soldiers found putrid. (2.11.2)

Thought: Not only is Billy a pretty sad soldier to start with – since we know he is funny-looking and scrawny – but his job in the army is not even a combatant position. He ministers to men who don't believe in his religion. Billy is absolutely unsuited to be in war, and yet he's still there. Fate?

Little Billy was terrified, because his father had said Billy was going to learn to swim by the method of sink-or-swim. His father was going to throw Billy into the deep end, and Billy was going to damn well swim.

It was like an execution. . . . [Billy] dimly sensed that somebody was rescuing him. Billy resented that. (2.25.5)

Thought: When Billy has his mental breakdown after the war, his doctors trace it back to this traumatic moment in the swimming pool. While we think Billy's breakdown probably has a *little* something to do with the war, we do agree that this scene represents pretty much everything that's wrong with Billy's life in miniature. He has no choice about being tossed into the pool and he has no choice about being saved from it – much like he has no choice but to go fight in

the Battle of the Bulge, and he has no choice but to keep going afterwards.

The dog, who had sounded so ferocious in the winter distances, was a female German shepherd. She was shivering. Her tail was between her legs. She had been borrowed that morning from a farmer. She had never been to war before. She had no idea what game was being played. Her name was Princess. (3.1.2)

Thought: Much like Billy himself, Princess was drafted into this war and is pretty unhappy about it. The cold, impersonal way in which both Billy and Princess get put into situations that makes them uncomfortable really highlights the fact that war is about the *opposite* of free will. Very few people in this novel have any kind of choice in determining their own lives.

Among the things Billy Pilgrim could not change were the past, the present, and the future. (3.13.2)

Thought: This would seem to suggest that Billy is subject to fate. He cannot change what has already happened to him, what is happening to him, or what will happen to him. This is in part because he is an enlisted man, but also because he is a fictional character – he literally has no free will. How does the narrator show more self-determination and free will than Billy?

The saucer was one hundred feet in diameter, with portholes around its rim. The light from the portholes was a pulsing purple. . . . Billy's will was paralyzed by a zap gun aimed at him from one of the portholes. It became imperative that he take hold of the bottom rung of the sinuous ladder, which he did. (4.6.1-2)

Thought: Much like the Germans, the Tralfamadorians take away all of Billy's choices. So why does Billy seem to embrace the Tralfamadorians and their point of view? And how does Billy's experience of captivity seem to differ from Montana Wildhack's? Are her range of choices the same as Billy's?

"Why you? Why us for that matter? Why anything? Because this moment simply is. Have you ever seen bugs trapped in amber? . . . Well, here we are, Mr. Pilgrim, trapped in the amber of this moment. There is no why." (4.7.4-6)

Thought: What do you think of this idea that there is no need to explain anything, because it simply *is*? Why is Billy so pleased to give up on the whole idea of free will?

"Why me?" he asked the guard.

The guard shoved him back into ranks. "Vy you? Vy anybody?" he said. (5.9.3-4)

Thought: This exchange takes place when an American soldier says something in English that a German guard overhears and finds offensive. The German soldier punches the American, apparently out of the blue. But this dialogue is also reminiscent of the Tralfamadorians' words to Billy Pilgrim: "Why *you*? Why *us* for that matter?" (4.7.4). This question of "why" seems to be one the narrator is asking the universe at large. *Why* do some people suffer so much and others don't? Billy's answer is the Tralfamadorian abandonment of free will. Does the novel offer any other answers? Are there any other answers *to* offer?

"If you know [that the Universe will be destroyed by a Tralfamadorian pilot who presses a button]," said Billy, "isn't there some way you can prevent it? Can't you keep the pilot from pressing the button?"

"He has always pressed it, and he always will. We always let him and we always will let him. The moment is structured that way." (5.44.1-2)

Thought: What kinds of ethical problems does this Tralfamadorian perspective on fate seem to present? Are these ethical problems applicable to Billy and his own choices? If so, how?

Billy found two small sources [of animal magnetism], two lumps an inch apart and hidden in the lining [of his jacket]. One was shaped like a pea. The other was shaped like a tiny horseshoe. Billy received a message carried by the radiation. He was told not to find out what the lumps were. He was advised to be content with knowing that they could work miracles for him, provided he did not insist on learning their nature. That was all right with Billy Pilgrim. He was grateful. He was glad. (6.1.7)

Thought: This whole bit about animal magnetism is odd, to say the least, and it's one of the few moments when the narrator refuses to explain something. In fact, the two lumps are a diamond (which Billy gives to Valencia after the war) and a partial denture (which Billy keeps in a box). The source of their power remains completely obscure. But we find it interesting that Billy is totally satisfied that "they could work miracles for him, provided he did not insist on learning their nature." Billy has no curiosity; he just wants to go along and get along. Perhaps this provides one explanation for why he is OK with the idea that he has no free will: he never, ever wants to make choices or rock the boat.

Warfare Quotes

Do you know what I say to people when I hear they're writing anti-war books? . . . I say, 'Why don't you write an anti-glacier book instead?' (1.2.9-11)

Thought: These are the words of real-life director Harrison Starr to the narrator in Chapter 1. Billy Pilgrim spends most of *Slaughterhouse-Five* trying to survive when he has no control over his own life. Interestingly, the narrator himself seems to be struggling with a similar conceptual problem: how should he write a book against something he is pretty sure will never change? After all, if war and violence are part of human nature, how is Vonnegut supposed to imagine an alternative? But he tries, which is what distinguishes his character from Billy's.

You were just babies in the war – like the ones upstairs! . . . But you're not going to write it that way, are you. . . . You'll pretend you were men instead of babies, and you'll be played in the movies by Frank Sinatra and John Wayne or some of those other glamorous, war-loving, dirty old men. And war will look just wonderful, so we'll have a lot more of them. And they'll be fought by babies like the babies upstairs. (1.10.13-18)

Thought: Mary O'Hare thinks wars continue to be popular because writers glamorize the soldier's life. To counteract these kinds of stories, *Slaughterhouse-Five* is about the least glamorous account of life as a soldier you can imagine.

I have told my sons that they are not under any circumstances to take part in massacres, and that the news of massacres of enemies is not to fill them with satisfaction or glee. (1.16.1)

Billy's son Robert had a lot of trouble in high school, but then he joined the famous Green Berets. He straightened out, became a fine young man, and he fought in Vietnam. (2.4.1)

Thought: How does the narrator's treatment of his sons differ from Billy's treatment of Robert Pilgrim? Which do you think is the more ethically responsible? And why does Billy offer so little insight into Robert's character? He seems completely estranged from both his children. All this about Robert "straightening out and becoming a fine young man" reads more like a movie summary than a real assessment by a caring father of his son's character.

Weary's version of the true war story went like this. There was a big German attack, and Weary and his antitank buddies fought like hell until everybody was killed but Weary. So it goes. And then Weary tied in with two scouts, and they became close friends immediately, and they decided to fight their way back to their own lines. They were going to travel fast. They were damned if they'd surrender. They shook hands all around. They called themselves "The Three Musketeers." (2.24.3)

Thought: Even as Weary is in the middle of a real war, he fantasizes about what the war *should* be like. It's stories like Weary's that terrify and anger Mary O'Hare in the first chapter of the book. What does the novel suggest motivates Weary's bullying behavior? How does Weary's upbringing compare to Billy's? Do the differences between the two explain the differences in their characters?

The Germans and the dog were engaged in a military operation which had an amusingly self-explanatory name, a human enterprise which is seldom described in detail, whose name alone, when reported as news or history, gives many war enthusiasts a sort of post-coital satisfaction. It is, in the imagination of combat's fans, the divinely listless loveplay that follows the orgasm of victory. It is called "mopping up." (3.1.1)

Thought: Whoa, there's a lot of sexual imagery in this description of "mopping up" a battlefield. And Montana Wildhack describes Edgar Derby's execution much later in the novel as a "blue movie" – a pornographic film (9.33). Why does the narrator seem to connect war and violence with sex?

But the colonel imagined that he was addressing his beloved troops for the last time, and he told them that they had nothing to be ashamed of, that there were dead Germans all over the battlefield who wished to God they had never heard of the Four-fifty-first. . . .

He said all this while staring into Billy's eyes. He made the inside of poor Billy's skull echo with balderdash. (3.25.3-4)

Thought: What is the "balderdash" that Wild Bob is spouting here? What kind of comments might the narrator be making about Wild Bob's heroic speech to his imagined regiment?

When the beautiful people were past, Valencia questioned her funny-looking husband about war. It was a simple-minded thing for a female Earthling to do, to associate sex and glamor with war. (5.50.1)

Thought: It's not just male war buffs who associate war with sex or who get some kind of pornographic excitement from violence. (See our quote from Chapter 3 above for more on this.) Valencia is also getting kind of excited at the idea that Billy was in a war. But what do you make of the description of this association as "a simple-minded thing for a female Earthling"?

You needn't worry about bombs, by the way. Dresden is an open city. It is undefended, and contains no war industries or troop concentrations of any importance. (6.14.6)

Thought: This line is delivered by the British colonel, who still seems to have faith that all the violence in the war is fair, justified, and aimed at appropriate wartime targets. Yet, as we know, Billy and his POW comrades are anything but safe as they travel to Dresden. How does the colonel's ideas of warfare differ from the reality of Billy Pilgrim's experiences on the ground in Germany?

Trout's leading robot looked like a human being, and could talk and dance and so on, and go out with girls. And nobody held it against him that he dropped jellied gasoline on people. But they found his halitosis unforgivable. But then he cleared that up, and he was welcomed to the human race. (8.8.5)

Thought: Kilgore Trout's novel suggests that people care more about how you look, dress, and smell than about what you do in the middle of a war. Do you think this is true? Do we see any similar criticism of social codes in other parts of the book?

Time Quotes

Time obsessed [Céline]. Miss Ostrovsky reminded me of the amazing scene in Death on the Installment Plan where Céline wants to stop the bustling of a street crowd. He screams on paper, Make them stop . . . don't let them move anymore at all . . . There, make them freeze . . . once and for all! . . . So that they won't disappear anymore! (1.20.3)

Thought: We can't help but notice a *striking* similarity between Céline's desire to stop time to keep people from dying and Billy Pilgrim's decision that time can never change, so people never really die. How does Vonnegut use other fictional and nonfictional sources to build his novel?

Billy is spastic in time, has no control over where he is going next, and the trips aren't necessarily fun. He is in a constant state of stage fright, he says, because he never knows what part of his life he is going to have to act in next. (2.1.5)

Thought: Billy has not just lost control over the most fundamental constant we come to expect in life – time. He also feels phony in performing his own life. This lack of conviction about who he is makes Billy a nontraditional hero for a novel. Who in the novel *does* have a strong sense of self? And is this necessarily a *good* thing to have?

The most important thing I learned on Tralfamadore was that when a person dies he only appears to die. He is still very much alive in the past, so it is very silly for people to cry at his funeral. All moments, past, present, and future, always have existed, always will exist. (2.7.2)

Thought: Even if it's true that death is only a fleeting moment in a person's life, are human beings capable of experiencing another person's death this way? Is it possible for us not to cry at funerals? Does Billy's philosophy have any resonance or meaning for you?

When a Tralfamadorian sees a corpse, all he thinks is that the dead person is in bad condition in that particular moment, but that the same person is just fine in plenty of other moments. Now, when I myself hear that somebody is dead, I simply shrug and say what the Tralfamadorians say about dead people, which is 'So it goes.' (2.7.3)

Thought: If we could live life out of order and pick and choose what to experience, could we learn anything from the past? Is *Slaughterhouse-Five* trying to *teach* anything, or is it simply an effort to represent a series of conflicting ideas?

Billy Pilgrim had stopped in the forest. He was leaning against a tree with his eyes closed. His head was tilted back and his nostrils were flaring. He was like a poet in the Parthenon.

This was when Billy first came unstuck in time. His attention began to swing grandly through the full arc of his life, passing into death, which was violet light. There wasn't anybody else there, or anything. There was just violet light – and a hum. (2.25.1-2)

Thought: For the first time, as Billy is faced with the possibility of his own death, he sees his life *literally* flashing before his eyes. How does the book take the idea of traumatic flashbacks and run with it? What purpose does Billy's time travel serve in *Slaughterhouse-Five*?

[Billy is watching a war movie in reverse.]

When the [American] bombers got back to their base, the steel cylinders were taken from the racks and shipped back to the United States of America, where factories were operating night and day, dismantling the cylinders, separating the dangerous contents into minerals . . .

The American fliers turned in their uniforms, became high school kids. And Hitler turned into a baby, Billy Pilgrim supposed. That wasn't in the movie. Billy was extrapolating. Everybody turned into a baby, and all humanity, without exception, conspired biologically to produce two perfect people named Adam and Eve, he supposed. (4.4.1-2)

Thought: Billy imagines going back to a time before the war. But to go back far enough to avoid pain and suffering, you'd have to go all the way back to Adam and Eve. Again, war seems to be part of human nature, and how do we fight that?

"I am a Tralfamadorian, seeing all time as you might see a stretch of the Rocky Mountains. All time is all time. It does not change. It does not lend itself to warnings or explanations. It simply is. Take it moment by moment, and you will find that we are all, as I've said before, bugs in amber."

"You sound to me as though you don't believe in free will," said Billy Pilgrim. (4.21.5-6)

Thought: Free will depends on a progressive notion of time, in which we proceed from past to present to future. Without an infinite future in front of us, we cannot choose to change anything – we have no free will. Yet, in reality, even if we do live in time, as humans are supposed to, we still struggle against constraints on our freedom. We cannot choose to make a kajillion dollars just because we want to, for example. Thus, while free will depends on a sequential notion of time, having time in front of you does not guarantee freedom.

Billy thought hard about the effect the quartet had had on him, and then found an association with an experience he had had long ago. He did not travel in time to the experience. He remembered it shimmeringly. (8.22.1)

Thought: This scene with the barbershop quartet is one of the only moments in the book when Billy *remembers* the past instead of *reliving* it. We think this is because he is not recalling an actual barbershop quartet like the one in front of him. Instead, he associates barbershop quartets with the German guards seeing the devastation of Dresden for the first time. How does the emotional impact of Billy's memories differ from his time travel?

On Tralfamadore, says Billy Pilgrim, there isn't much interest in Jesus Christ. The Earthling figure who is most engaging to the Tralfamadorian mind, he says, is Charles Darwin – who taught that those who die are meant to die, that corpses are improvements. (10.2.1)

Thought: Darwin's idea of evolution teaches that species die out for a reason. But in a sense, it seems odd that the Tralfamadorians would appreciate this idea, because they deliberately refuse to ask the question Darwin answers: "Why?"

Suffering Quotes

Billy says that he first came unstuck in time in 1944, long before his trip to Tralfamadore. The Tralfamadorians didn't have anything to do with his coming unstuck. They were simply able to give him insights into what was really going on. (2.11.1)

Thought: So the novel clearly distinguishes between the cure for Billy's existential angst – the Tralfamadorians – and whatever caused him to become unstuck from time. Billy's time travel appears to be a symptom of his overall suffering. The moment he truly begins to realize he is in deadly danger behind enemy lines, he flashes forward beyond death, back before birth, and then to the moment when he almost drowned trying to learn to swim.

Billy, after all, had contemplated torture and hideous wounds at the beginning and the end of nearly every day of his childhood. Billy had an extremely gruesome crucifix hanging on the wall of his little bedroom in Ilium. A military surgeon would have admired the clinical fidelity of the artist's rendition of all Christ's wounds – the spear wound, the thorn wounds, the holes that were made by the iron spikes. Billy's Christ died horribly. He was pitiful. (2.19.15)

Thought: One reason Billy does not seem to seek comfort in God (even though he is a chaplain's assistant before he is taken captive by the Germans) is that he associates Christianity with a suffering Christ. Billy himself is frequently compared to Christ – in the epigraph and because of his job in the army – so why would he seek solace in a religion that is OK with his suffering?

Weary drew back his right boot, aimed a kick at the spine, at the tube which had so many of Billy's important wires in it. Weary was going to break that tube.

But then Weary saw that he had an audience. Five German soldiers and a police dog on a leash were looking down into the bed of the creek. The soldiers' blue eyes were filled with a bleary civilian curiosity as to why one American would try to murder another one so far from home, and why the victim should laugh. (2.33.6-7)

Thought: Billy isn't really laughing, though it looks that way; he's actually convulsing. Why does Weary decide to add to Billy's suffering by bullying him *on the battlefield* when they are *both in danger*? What does this say about Weary's character?

[Billy] was under doctor's orders to take a nap every day. The doctor hoped that this would relieve a complaint that Billy had: Every so often, for no apparent reason, Billy Pilgrim would find himself weeping. Nobody had ever caught Billy doing it. Only the doctor knew. It was an extremely quiet thing Billy did, and not very moist. (3.15.1)

Thought: The reason for Billy's weeping may not be apparent to the doctor, but is it apparent to us? Beyond Billy's war experiences, what else might he have to cry about?

And now there was an acrimonious madrigal, with parts sung in all quarters of the car. Nearly everybody, seemingly, had an atrocity story of something Billy Pilgrim had done to him in his sleep. Everybody told Billy Pilgrim to keep the hell away. (4.9.16)

Thought: An "acrimonious madrigal" in this context is a loud, furious, multipart harmony of people yelling at Billy. No one in the POW train car wants to sleep next to Billy because he whimpers and kicks so badly in his sleep. Why does no one *ever* show any sympathy for Billy's suffering? How do you respond to Billy's *extreme* portrayal as helpless and childlike? How might this portrayal fit into other themes such as fate and free will or men and masculinity?

Billy looked inside the latrine. The wailing was coming from in there. The place was crammed with Americans who had taken their pants down. The welcome feast had made them as sick as volcanoes. The buckets were full or had been kicked over.

An American near Billy wailed that he had excreted everything but his brains. Moments later he said, "There they go, there they go." He meant his brains. (5.53-6-7)

Thought: War stories often contain descriptions of wounds, but this book has little time for wartime casualties. We *do*, however, get a lot of illness: Weary's gangrene, Wild Bob's fever, and the soldiers' diarrhea here, to name a few. This focus on the suffering of the *sick* human body really underlines the physical exhaustion and depravation these POWs must cope with throughout the novel. Also, by focusing on diarrhea instead of, say, a bullet wound, Vonnegut is once again drawing the reader's mind away from any kind of battlefield heroism.

So Billy made a [syrup] lollipop for [Edgar Derby]. He opened the window. He stuck the lollipop into poor old Derby's gaping mouth. A moment passed, and then Derby burst into tears. (7.11.2)

Thought: Edgar Derby, who has been the strongest of the American POWs throughout the whole book, is reduced to tears by the taste of syrup in his mouth after so much hunger. Again, this novel really takes the romance out of warfare and exposes the incredible deprivation that war really brings to the men fighting it.

Nobody talked much as the expedition crossed the moon. There was nothing appropriate to say. One thing was clear: Absolutely everybody in the city was supposed to be dead, regardless of what they were, and that anybody that moved in it represented a flaw in the design. There were to be no moon men at all. (8.26.2)

Thought: From a distance, from the perspective of the American fighter planes flying over Dresden, no one can be allowed to live. The pilot doesn't know whether he is shooting German soldiers, civilians, or even Americans. This kind of detached perspective on killing is what makes massacres like Dresden possible. Even someone as cold and callous as Bertram Copeland Rumfoord recognizes that it must have been especially hard for Billy to experience Dresden's firestorm at ground level.

The Maori Billy had worked with died of the dry heaves, after having been ordered to go down in that stink and work. He tore himself to pieces, throwing up and throwing up. (10.10.3)

Thought: Even without being injured directly, the presence of so much death is so incompatible with life that it kills this Maori soldier from the inside out.

Morality and Ethics Quotes

I happened to tell a University of Chicago professor at a cocktail party about the raid as I had seen it, about the book I would write. He was a member of a thing called The Committee on Social Thought. And he told me about the concentration camps, and about how the Germans had made soap and candles out of the fat of dead Jews and so on.

All I could say was, "I know, I know. I know." (1.6.2-3)

Thought: We can imagine someone justifying the firestorm of Dresden by saying, look, it's *quid pro quo*: the Germans were *exterminating people*, and the war had to be stopped as quickly as possible. But Vonnegut witnessed the deaths of thousands of noncombatants. He wants to find a way to talk about that experience, even though he knows that, as a country, Germany did terrible things during the war. So he raises the concentration camps to say that, yes, he knows – but still, aside from larger questions of morality, he saw the boiled bodies of schoolgirls. What could make that right or correct?

Those were vile people in both those cities [Sodom and Gomorrah], as is well known. The world was better off without them.

And Lot's wife, of course, was told not to look back where all those people and their homes had been. But she did look back, and I love her for that, because it was so human. (1.21.3-4)

Thought: By comparing himself to Lot's wife, the narrator acknowledges, again, that Germany bore a lot of guilt for what was happening in the war. But that does not mean that it is not *human* and *necessary* to bear witness to the suffering of ordinary Germans, as witnessed by Vonnegut himself.

There was a tap on Billy's car window. A black man was out there. He wanted to talk about something. The light had changed. Billy did the simplest thing. He drove on. (3.9.2)

Thought: Who knows what this man was going to say to Billy? Billy never will, because he refuses to listen. We get hints throughout the novel that Billy is not particularly compassionate, as when he sees a pair of disabled men trying to sell magazine subscriptions and refuses to answer the doorbell. When does Billy start trying to comfort the suffering of others? Why?

Billy was not moved to protest the bombing of North Vietnam, did not shudder about the hideous things he himself had seen bombing do. He was simply having lunch with the Lions Club, of which he was past president now. (3.12.1)

Thought: Why might Billy be unable to apply his own experiences of massacres and death to contemporary politics? How does his belief that people have no free will affect his ability to learn any lessons from his past?

Only the candles and the soap were of German origin. They had a ghostly, opalescent similarity. The British had no way of knowing it, but the candles and the soap were made from the fat of rendered Jews and Gypsies and fairies and communists, and other enemies of the State. (5.14.4)

Thought: This is a particularly awful example of something that comes up again and again throughout the book: people often benefit from the suffering of others without knowing it. Another example is the suffering horses in Chapter 9 (see our "Symbols, Imagery, Allegory" section). Can we hold the British officers responsible for using human soap and candles? Of course they don't know they are doing so – but they are also not bothering to find out. They are willing to stay ignorant and comfortable in their own compound, and none of them seem eager to disturb their status quo with the Germans.

The flaw in the Christ stories, said the visitor from outer space, was that Christ, who didn't look like much, was actually the Son of the Most Powerful Being in the Universe. Readers understood that, so, when they came to the crucifixion, they naturally thought, and Rosewater read out loud again:

Oh boy – they sure picked the wrong guy to lynch that time!

And that thought had a brother: "There are right people to lynch." Who? People not well connected. So it goes. (5.31.2-3)

Thought: Kilgore Trout often criticizes Christian theology for not doing enough to prevent human suffering. And despite having been a chaplain's assistant, Billy does not turn to Christ for comfort. What kinds of general comments or criticism might *Slaughterhouse-Five* be making about the Christian faith? What does Vonnegut propose in its place?

On other days we have wars as horrible as any you've ever seen or read about. There isn't anything we can do about them, so we simply don't look at them. We ignore them. We spend eternity looking at pleasant moments – like today at the zoo. (5.45.4)

Thought: Is the Tralfamadorian stance on war – that "we simply don't look at them" – morally viable? Does the book seem to offer an opinion about Tralfamadorian ideas of morality? If so, where and what is it?

"[Revenge] is the sweetest thing there is," said Lazzaro. "People fuck with me," he said, "and Jesus Christ are they ever fucking sorry. I laugh like hell. I don't care if it's a guy or a dame. If the President of the United States fucked around with me, I'd fix him good." (6.3.2)

Thought: Lazzaro has his own messed up moral code: if you do him wrong, he'll get revenge. The obvious problem with his code is that he is a nutcase, so he *always* thinks people are doing him wrong, whether they mean to or not.

"You're going to have to fight the Communists sooner or later," said Campbell. "Why not get it over with now?" (8.3.3)

Thought: Howard W. Campbell, Jr. is a fictional American Nazi who leaves the United States for Germany because he thinks Americans hate the poor. Whatever you may think of this suggestion, his primary appearance in this book is to try to convince the American POWs to join the German army to fight a common enemy. He is preaching expediency: the end justifies the means.

"[Dresden] was all right," said Billy. "Everything is all right, and everybody has to do exactly what he does. I learned that on Tralfamadore." (9.22.10)

Thought: Billy has found a way to make everything that has happened in his life seem OK: faith in Tralfamadore. What else has he tried to assuage the pain? Christianity (as a chaplain's assistant), money (he's making bank as an optometrist), and family (he marries a girl he doesn't like that much because he feels he needs to). But when all else fails, Billy goes for Tralfamadore.

Foolishness and Folly Quotes

Billy was preposterous – six feet and three inches tall, with a chest and shoulders like a box of kitchen matches. He had no helmet, no overcoat, no weapon, and no boots. On his feet were cheap, low-cut civilian shoes which he had bought for his father's funeral. Billy had lost a heel, which made him bob up-and-down-up-and-down. The involuntary dancing, up-and-down, up-and-down, made his hip joints sore. (2.13.4)

Thought: Oh, hey, check it out – a reference to the title! Or anyway, the subtitle ("A Duty-Dance With Death"). Billy Pilgrim is completely, totally unprepared for war, with his poor physique, lack of gear, and messed up shoes. But still, he is going, because he has to: his dance with death has begun. And this dance is *involuntary*. As a soldier, Billy has no choice but to follow his orders, no matter how utterly ill-equipped he is for the battlefield. Billy may look like an idiot – or "preposterous," as the narrator calls him – but the real idiots are the guys back home who deployed him to the front lines of a war.

Billy stood there politely, giving the marksman another chance. It was his addled understanding of the rules of warfare that the marksman should be given a second chance. The next shot missed Billy's kneecaps by inches, going end-on-end, from the sound of it. (2.14.2)

Thought: Again, we cannot say enough about what a complete idiot Billy is. He is so naive that he doesn't know better than to *get out of the way of a bullet coming in his direction*. Billy wants to do the right thing, but he is so utterly turned around that he has completely lost track of what that "right thing" might be.

Weary told Billy about neat tortures he'd read about or seen in the movies or heard on the radio – about other neat tortures he himself had invented. (2.18.3)

Thought: Behind enemy lines, trying to escape German soldiers, Weary spends his energy telling Billy about torture. While Billy may be terribly naive, he at least is aware of his own vulnerability to the war going on around him.

Billy Pilgrim dressed himself. He put on the little overcoat, too. It split up the back, and, at the shoulders, the sleeves came entirely free. So the coat became a fur-collared vest. It was meant to flare at its owner's waist, but the flaring took place at Billy's armpits. The Germans found him to be one of the most screamingly funny things they had seen in all of World War II. They laughed and laughed. (5.7.3)

Thought: One thing you can say about Billy is that he is completely unselfconscious. He spends much of the war looking like a fool, in a too-small coat, a blue curtain, and silver boots. But he keeps on going. Billy goes on looking like an idiot and surviving where other, self-consciously idealistic men die. We can compare him with men like Weary, who is so well equipped that he overestimates his own strength against the Germans, and Edgar Derby, who keeps up his physique and is relatively worldly wise, but still manages to get shot at the end of the war.

There at the corner, in the front rank of pedestrians, was a surgeon who had been operating all day. He was a civilian, but his posture was military. He had served in two world wars. The sight of Billy offended him, especially after he learned from the guards that Billy was an American. It seemed to him that Billy was in abominable taste, supposed that Billy had gone to a lot of silly trouble to costume himself just so.

The surgeon spoke English, and he said to Billy, "I take it you find war a very comical thing." (6.21.1-2)

Thought: No one can believe that Billy could look the way he does unintentionally. But pretty much nothing he does is intentional. He has no idea what to do or even where he is half the time. Is there ever a moment in the novel in which Billy seems to care about his appearance? When and why?

Billy Pilgrim got onto a chartered airplane in Ilium twenty-five years after [going to Slaughterhouse-Five]. He knew it was going to crash, but he didn't want to make a fool of himself by saying so. (7.1.1)

Thought: Billy claims to know his plane is going to crash, but he doesn't want to look like a fool by saying so. If he really did know, Billy could have saved a lot of lives, including his father-in-law's, by being willing to look like a fool. Billy survives the war by being lucky (and unselfconscious). When does he suddenly start to feel embarrassed or ashamed of himself?

[The stock tickers and telephones] were simply stimulants to make the Earthlings perform vividly for the crowds at the zoo – to make them jump up and down and cheer, or gloat, or sulk, or tear their hair, to be scared shitless or to feel contented as babies in their mothers' arms. (9.27.2)

Thought: This is a passing description of one of Kilgore Trout's novels, about a man and a woman in an alien zoo who are made to perform for the amusement of the aliens thanks to a bunch of fake stock information. When they think they have made money, they celebrate; when they think they have lost money, they get depressed. But there *is* no real money. This seems comparable to the deluded dreams of Roland Weary, who firmly believes he is fighting a winning battle even as he is running around behind enemy lines just waiting to become a

prisoner of war. The human ability to believe something against all evidence to the contrary seems pretty foolish to us.

Freedom and Confinement Quotes

[Roland Weary] had been saving Billy's life for days, cursing him, kicking him, slapping him, making him move. It was absolutely necessary that cruelty be used, because Billy wouldn't do anything to save himself. Billy wanted to quit. He was cold, hungry, embarrassed, incompetent. He could scarcely distinguish between sleep and wakefulness now, on the third day, found no important differences, either, between walking and standing still. (2.15.1)

Thought: The definition of freedom in this book goes beyond freedom from POW camps. Here, Billy is completely under the power of Roland Weary, who insists on saving his life even though Billy wants to die. The problem with being under someone's power like that, even someone who is saving your life, is that you have no choice if he suddenly changes his mind. When Weary turns on Billy, Billy has absolutely no defense against him.

The [German] photographer wanted something more lively, though, a picture of an actual capture. So the guards staged one for him. They threw Billy into shrubbery. When Billy came out of the shrubbery, his face wreathed in goofy good will, they menaced him with their machine pistols, as though they were capturing him then. (3.7.3)

Thought: Again, Billy has no idea what he is in the middle of. He goes along with the Germans throwing him into a bush the same way he goes along with Weary in the preceding passages. Billy seems to have a gift for submission: he's just looking for people to tell him what to do.

The [Americans] came to a shed where a corporal with only one arm and one eye wrote the name and serial number of each prisoner in a big, red ledger. Everybody was legally alive now. Before they got their names and numbers in that book, they were missing in action and probably dead. (5.8.1)

Thought: There's a level of bureaucracy to this whole life, death, and freedom question that keeps coming up throughout the novel. Billy's squad is reported killed before they are even sent to Europe, and the British compound of the POW camp is kept amazingly well-stocked with supplies thanks to bureaucratic mix-ups. Billy only comes to back to "life" after going missing in action when the Germans log him as an official prisoner of war.

Billy covered his head with his blanket again. He always covered his head when his mother came to see him in the mental ward – always got much sicker until she went away. . . .

She upset Billy simply by being his mother. She made him feel embarrassed and ungrateful and weak because she had gone to so much trouble to give him life, and to keep that life going, and Billy didn't really like life at all. (5.23.3-4)

Thought: Another form of confinement we find in the book involves Billy's complicated relationship with family. He seems to view family as another duty he has to fulfill: he makes money to improve the Pilgrim family name and he marries Valencia because he seems to feel he has no choice. But we get very little insight into how he feels about his family. When he's in the hospital trying to escape from life, his family just seems like yet another prison he has to deal with.

So the Americans put their weapons down, and they came out of the woods with their hands on top of their heads, because they wanted to go on living if they possibly could. (5.27.14)

Thought: This line appears in an account of Edgar Derby's capture by the Germans. Even though much of the book seems to be about the possibility of escaping various literal and metaphoric prisons, life is still usually more appealing than death.

Billy didn't want to marry ugly Valencia. She was one of the symptoms of his disease. He knew he was going crazy when he heard himself proposing marriage to her, when he begged her to take the diamond ring and be his companion for life. (5.28.4)

Thought: Marriage is just another layer of confinement in Billy's life. And yet, he never considers *not* marrying Valencia despite his family's wishes. How much responsibility should Billy bear for his own loss of freedom? What would Billy do with real freedom if he had it?

Billy was displayed [on Tralfamadore] in the zoo in a simulated Earthling habitat. Most of the furnishings had been stolen from the Sears Roebuck warehouse in Iowa City, Iowa. (5.38.1)

Thought: Billy is happier in captivity on Tralfamadore than he is back on Earth, even though he is naked and exposed to the gazes of aliens who want him to perform for their amusement. What's to like about this situation? How does Billy describe his confinement? How does his confinement sound to you – like good times?

"Did you hear what I said?" Barbara inquired. It was 1968 again.

"Of course." [Billy] had been dozing.

"If you're going to act like a child, maybe we'll just have to treat you like a child." (5.59.1-3)

Thought: Barbara is really getting off on this power trip over her old man, we'd say. In what sense does aging seem like another kind of confinement? Billy has various encounters with aging people: his dying mother (2.26) and an old man in a doctor's waiting room (9.19). How does Vonnegut represent aging?

You lads are leaving this afternoon for Dresden – a beautiful city, I'm told. You won't be cooped up like us. You'll be out where the life is, and the food is certain to be more plentiful than here. If I may inject a personal note: It has been five years now since I have seen a tree or flower or woman or child – or a dog or a cat or a place of entertainment, or a human being doing useful work of any kind. (6.14.5)

Thought: Note how the British colonel represents his own feelings of confinement. He is perfectly comfortable and warm in the compound, but he misses activity and social community. In fact, Billy's postwar life seems a little like this, except that his captivity isn't quite as obvious. Billy, too, is physically comfortable and well provided for, but he doesn't get to make choices about where to go or what to do with his life. All those choices are made by his family and social circumstances.

Poor old Derby, the doomed high school teacher, lumbered to his feet for what was probably the finest moment in his life. There are almost no characters in this story, and almost no dramatic confrontations, because most of the people in it are so sick and so much the listless playthings of enormous forces. One of the main effects of war, after all, is that people are discouraged from being characters. But old Derby was a character now. . . .

Derby raised his head, called Campbell a snake. He corrected that. He said that snakes couldn't help being snakes, and that Campbell, who could help being what he was, was something much lower than a snake or a rat – or even a blood-filled tick. (8.4.1-2)

Thought: Derby is one of the very few characters in the novel, with the possible exception of post-Tralfamadore Billy, who actually takes some initiative. He is in captivity, just like all the other men in this POW camp, but his mind is still actively considering right and wrong. It is this taking of initiative that makes Derby seem like a real person, or a "character."

Men and Masculinity Quotes

A German measured Billy's upper right arm with his thumb and forefinger, asked a companion what sort of an army would send a weakling like that to the front. They looked at other American bodies now, pointed out a lot more that were nearly as bad as Billy's. (4.17.5)

Thought: Not only is Vonnegut seriously challenging all the heroic stereotypes of the war genre; he is also specifically criticizing the idea that *American* bodies are the best in the world. These patriotic stereotypes get turned on their ears in *Slaughterhouse-Five*, where nearly all the American soldiers are pretty busted. As America throws more troops at World War II, many of the recruits are too young, too old, or not athletic enough to be there. Still, war demands bodies, no matter what they look like.

The Englishmen were clean and enthusiastic and decent and strong. They sang boomingly well. They had been singing together every night for years.

The Englishmen had also been lifting weights and chinning themselves for years. Their bellies were like washboards. The muscles of their calves and upper arms were like cannonballs. They were all masters of checkers and chess and bridge and cribbage and dominoes and anagrams and charades and Ping-Pong and billiards, as well. (5.12.5)

Thought: The Englishmen have been living in captivity for years, eating and resting and staying warm. Meanwhile, the rest of Europe has been suffering and dying. There is a total irony here: the people who are actually fighting the war are ill-equipped boys, and the men who wish they were fighting the war are all cooped up in this compound in the middle of a German prison for Russians.

Most Tralfamadorians had no way of knowing Billy's body and face were not beautiful. They supposed that he was a splendid specimen. This had a pleasant effect on Billy, who began to enjoy his body for the first time. (5.40.1)

Thought: Everything is relative. The only reason everyone thinks Billy looks like a clownish, unattractive fellow is because we have billions of other humans to compare him to. Billy also loves to conform to other people's ideas: when everyone thinks he looks like a fool during the war, he dresses like a clown. When the Tralfamadorians think he is a perfect specimen of manhood, he starts to groom himself and exercise.

The Tralfamadorians tried to give Billy clues that would help him to imagine sex in the invisible dimension. They told him that there could be no Earthling babies without male homosexuals. There could be babies without female homosexuals. There couldn't be babies without women over sixty-five years old. The could be babies without men over sixty-five. There couldn't be

babies without other babies who had lived an hour or less after birth. And so on. (5.41.3)

Thought: We are really interested in this whole idea that babies need more than just one man and one woman to survive. They depend on a network of seven genders in ways we Earthlings can't understand, because we're blinded by our limited, three-dimensional view of the world. For one thing, it implies that there is no such thing as a superfluous or extra person: each individual human being is vital. Here is yet more evidence that Vonnegut is trying to counteract the idea that war or killing might sometimes, somehow be necessary.

A German major came in [to the camp hospital] now. He considered the Englishmen as close friends. He visited them nearly every day, played games with them, lectured to them on German history, played their piano, gave them lessons in conversational German. He told them often that, if it weren't for their civilized company, he would go mad. His English was splendid. (5.55.8)

Thought: The German major, like the Englishmen, sees very little real action outside their prison camp, so he has the luxury of befriending the English soldiers. They can all be gentlemen together. The reality of war is much crueler, as Billy learns when he sees the Dresden firestorm. These German-English relations seem to arise from an older ideal of war, in which both sides depend on mutual respect. By contrast, all of the bombing that allows the American Air Force to torch Dresden from the sky is the result of mutual ignorance, in which neither side is willing to admit to the humanity of the other.

Montana was naked, and so was Billy, of course. He had a tremendous wang, incidentally. You never know who'll get one. (5.61.2)

Thought: Throughout the book we've been told that Billy is a totally pathetic specimen of manhood. And yet, check it – he has a huge penis. Of course, Tralfamadore may just be Billy's fantasy land, so who knows, the penis may just be part of the dream.

In time, Montana came to love and trust Billy Pilgrim. He did not touch her until she made it clear that she wanted him to. After she had been on Tralfamadore for what would have been an Earthling week, she asked him shyly if he wouldn't sleep with her. Which he did. It was heavenly. (5.64.1)

Thought: This whole thing with Montana – don't even get us started. This idea that Montana would fall in love with Billy after a week is pretty hilarious. Billy wants to have sex with Montana, but he also wants to have at least a little bit of power over her, so he imagines waiting for her to come to him because she wants him so badly. After this whole book, in which Billy has been deprived of choice so many times, here he has his dream girl shyly asking *him* if *he* wants to

have sex with her, as though he'd be doing her a favor: a perfect fantasy.

What the Englishman said about survival was this: "If you stop taking pride in your appearance, you will very soon die." He said that he had seen several men die in the following way: "They ceased to stand up straight, then ceased to shave or wash, then ceased to get out of bed, then ceased to talk, then died." (6.13.1)

Thought: The narrator specifies several times that Billy has a straggly beard for much of his time as a POW – and yet he lives. Of course, he is not exactly the Englishman's model soldier. Perhaps a soldier of the English officer's kind would die from lack of self-respect, but Billy doesn't seem to have had much self-respect to start with.

[A kitchen worker near the slaughterhouse] asked [the German guard, Werner] Gluck if he wasn't awfully young to be in the army. He admitted that he was.

She asked Derby if he wasn't awfully old to be in the army. He said he was.

She asked Billy Pilgrim what he was supposed to be. Billy said he didn't know. He was just trying to keep warm. (7.9.3-5)

Thought: This is a kind of funny spin on the Goldilocks story: too young, too old, just wrong. All this surprise over Billy's physical condition emphasizes how shocking it is that he should be selected for survival among these much stronger, perhaps even more deserving men. And yet, he survives.

Rumfoord's left leg was in traction. He had broken it while skiing. He was seventy years old, but had the body and spirit of a man half that age. He had been honeymooning with his fifth wife when he broke his leg. Her name was Lily. Lily was twenty-three. (9.2.2)

Thought: Bertram Copeland Rumfoord is like Superman: he's wealthy, well-respected, loves war, and has a hot wife young enough to be his granddaughter. But he is a terrible person. Vonnegut does not seem to think much of hyper-violent, hyper-sexed masculinity.

Literature and Writing Quotes

All this happened, more or less. The war parts anyway, are pretty much true. One guy I knew really was shot in Dresden for taking a teapot that wasn't his. Another guy I knew really did threaten to have his personal enemies killed by hired gunmen after the war. And so on. I've changed all the names. (1.1.1)

Thought: If Vonnegut is writing a novel that is "pretty much true," why write it as fiction at all? What can fiction do that an autobiography can't? What kind of structural experimentation does writing about Dresden in a novel make possible?

I think of how useless the Dresden part of my memory has been, and yet how tempting Dresden has been to write about, and I am reminded of the famous limerick:

There was a young man from Stamboul,
Who soliloquized thus to his tool:
"You took all my wealth
And you ruined my health,
And now you won't pee, you old fool." (1.2.3-4)

Thought: First off, we think it's hilarious that the narrator starts off his quoting spree with a dirty limerick. Second, we find it intriguing that he feels almost compelled to write about Dresden, even though it's difficult, and even though it's taking up valuable real estate in his brain. How might writing itself be a form of therapy? What other reasons does the narrator give for needing to write about the Dresden firestorm? And what does this limerick mean, anyway?

"I think the climax of the book will be the execution of poor old Edgar Derby," I said. "The irony is so great. A whole city gets burned down, and thousands and thousands of people are killed. And then this one American foot soldier is arrested in the ruins for taking a teapot. And he's given a regular trial, and then he's shot by a firing squad." (1.3.19)

Thought: The narrator talks about Edgar Derby's real-life execution as though it were a moment of dramatic irony, as though the real war was also the product of an author with a dark sense of humor.

As a trafficker in climaxes and thrills and characterization and wonderful dialogue and suspense and confrontations, I had outlined the Dresden story many times. The best outline I ever made, or anyway, the prettiest one, was on the back of a roll of wallpaper. . . . The destruction of Dresden was represented by a vertical band of orange cross-hatching, and all the lines that were still alive passed through it, came out the other side. (1.4.2-3)

Thought: The narrator talks about writing 5,000 pages of his Dresden novel before actually getting to *Slaughterhouse-Five*. What makes the event so hard for him to write about? He describes the normal things that go into a novel – "climaxes and thrills and characterization and wonderful dialogue and suspense and confrontations" – none of which *Slaughterhouse-Five* actually has. Why might a book filled with these things be precisely *not* what the narrator wants to write when tackling the topic of war?

And what do the birds say? All there is to say about a massacre, things like "Poo-tee-weet?" (1.15.2)

Thought: The only sound left after a massacre is birdsong, so birds have the last word. Is this why the narrator also claims that his novel on Dresden must, inevitably, be a failure – because, in the end, there can simply be no words for such an event? Do you agree?

My other book was Erika Ostrovsky's Céline and his Vision. Céline was a brave French soldier in the First World War – until his skull was cracked. After that he couldn't sleep, and there were noises in his head. He became a doctor, and he treated poor people in the daytime, and he wrote grotesque novels all night. No art is possible without a dance with death, he wrote. (1.20.1)

Thought: We have been talking about the "dance with death" as something soldiers must do. They have to come to terms with the fact that they may die at any time, without warning. Still, the narrator specifically quotes Céline as saying that "no *art* is possible without a dance with death." Where do we see this dance with death in *Slaughterhouse-Five*?

"[E]ach clump of symbols is a brief, urgent message – describing a situation, a scene. We Tralfamadorians read them all at once, not one after the other. There isn't any particular relationship between all the messages, except that the author has chosen them carefully, so that, when seen all at once, they produce an image of life that is beautiful and surprising and deep. There is no beginning, no middle, no end, no suspense, no moral, no causes, no effects. (5.3.4)

Thought: *Slaughterhouse-Five* probably comes about as close as anything we have read to a novel with "no beginning, no middle, no end, [and] no suspense." Do you find that the lack of chronological order interferes with your understanding of the book?

[Rosewater] said that everything there was to know about life was in The Brothers Karamazov, by Feodor Dostoevsky. "But that isn't enough any more," said Rosewater. (5.21.1)

Thought: *The Brothers Karamazov* is a famous (and very long) realist novel that tackles themes of religion, family, crime, and punishment. Why does Rosewater feel that old stories involving these themes no longer describe the reality he and Billy live in?

"Did that really happen?" said Maggie White. She was a dull person, but a sensational invitation to make babies. . . .

"Of course it happened," Trout told her. "If I wrote something that hadn't really happened, and I tried to sell it, I could go to jail. That's fraud." (8.13.1-2)

Thought: Kilgore Trout is being facetious here by claiming that novelists are expected to write only the truth. At the same time, his novels, even if they are science fiction, tackle real and important subjects, such as greed, faith, and morality. With *Slaughterhouse-Five*, it seems to us that Vonnegut is claiming that many of the ideas expressed in fiction may not be literal or real, but they have a higher philosophical truth.

The master of ceremonies asked people to say what they thought the function of the novel might be in the modern society, and one critic said, "To provide touches of color in rooms with all-white walls." Another one said, "To describe blow-jobs artistically." Another one said, "To teach wives of junior executives what to buy next and how to act in a French restaurant." (9.32.1)

Thought: There really has been a discussion throughout much of the twentieth century about the so-called death of the novel. Many claim that authors have lost faith in the idea that a person can be conscious of what he does or why he does it, and that we also no longer believe in the rigid, formal presentation of fiction as though it is real. *Slaughterhouse-Five* itself experiments with new ways of presenting personal motivation and narrative time without throwing away the novel as a form. So we think Vonnegut is being kind of tongue-in-cheek here by showing all of these pretentious answers to a question about the value of the novel...inside a novel.

Plot Analysis

Classic Plot Analysis

We are faced with the problem that the whole plot of *Slaughterhouse-Five* goes out of order, so we get the "Complication Stage" of the plot – the firebombing of Dresden – *after* we see the effects of this firebombing on Billy's mental stability. So bear with us: we are going to map the progress of the plot as it happens chronologically but *not* as it unfolds in the novel itself.

Initial Situation

Billy Pilgrim goes to war.

In Chapter 2, we find out that our main character, Billy Pilgrim, is an optometry student in upstate New York who winds up getting drafted to join the army in 1944. He gets sent overseas to Luxembourg to fight the Germans in World War II, but he is taken prisoner nearly

immediately. This POW experience is the thing that sets up both his time travel and his eventual trips to the planet Tralfamadore.

Conflict

Billy becomes a prisoner of war.

We learn that Billy becomes a POW in the first sections of Chapter 2, but it isn't until Chapter 3 that we actually see him captured. Billy is carrying no weapons and is on the verge of being shot by fellow American soldier Roland Weary when the soldiers pick him up. Clearly, he is no one's idea of a hero. Billy is completely under the control of other people throughout the book, and his imprisonment is only the most exaggerated example of his lack of self-determination. Once Billy is taken prisoner, he starts skipping through time: he starts living life out of sequence because he has been so damaged by this initial experience.

Complication

Billy witnesses the firebombing of Dresden.

While the specter of Dresden hovers over the entire book, starting with the narrator's introduction in the first chapter, we do not actually see Billy's experience of it until Chapter 8. The sequence of events that change Billy's life forever – his being drafted and taken prisoner – really reach their peak here, when Billy survives the firebombing of Dresden. With no understanding of what is happening around him, Billy suddenly finds himself sheltering underground in a meat locker while an entire city goes up in flames above him.

Climax

Billy has a nervous breakdown after the war.

Billy returns to the U.S. three months after the February bombing, after being forced to dig through the ruins of Dresden looking for bodies. We know that Billy's return to upstate New York doesn't exactly mean that he has gone home: he is still skipping through time, and has been ever since he was taken prisoner.

A sense of unresolved mental pain fills Billy's whole story, but it really reaches its climax when he checks himself into a local veteran's hospital to recuperate in Chapter 5, Section 20. In conversation with Eliot Rosewater, another traumatized veteran, Billy learns to escape into the science fiction novels of Kilgore Trout. As the narrator comments, in the wake of all of this emotional suffering, "[Billy and Rosewater] were trying to re-invent themselves and their universe. Science fiction was a big help" (5.20.9).

Suspense

Billy recovers, but for how long?

We know that Billy goes on to live his life, because his story starts in Chapter 2 with the reassurance that after the war he will marry Valencia, have children, and become a successful, well-to-do optometrist. But we also know that he is going to tell the world about his travels to Tralfamadore and have a major falling-out with his daughter. It is not until Chapter 9 that we finally see the 1967 plane crash that seems to trigger Billy's decision to *do* something – for the

first time in his life – by telling the world about Tralfamadore. So we sit in suspense for many chapters before we find explanations for events that happen at the start of the novel.

Denouement

Billy begins telling the world that he has been abducted by aliens from the planet Tralfamadore. In Chapter 9, Billy finally comes to some kind of peace with his memories of the war, being held prisoner, and the Dresden firebombing. But this peace, oddly enough, seems to come once again from outside intervention: a freak plane crash leaves him telling the story of Tralfamadore for the first time. He informs Bertram Copeland Rumfoord: "*Everything* is all right, and everybody has to do exactly what he does. I learned that on Tralfamadore" (9.22.10). Billy has found a way to not blame anyone for the pain he has gone through: according to the Tralfamadorians, there is *no other way* that his life could have happened; there is no such thing as free will. This way of thinking comforts Billy after all of his unresolved pain about the war and his place in it.

Conclusion

Barbara Pilgrim takes Billy's responsibility for his own life away from him.
Ironically, the one thing that gives Billy comfort after he has been quietly suffering for 23 years with the memories of his capture and the massacre is also the thing that leads to his final loss of self-determination and self-control. When Billy sneaks out of the hospital where he has been recovering from his skull fracture in Chapter 9 and goes on the radio to talk about Tralfamadore, he gives his daughter all the reason she needs to believe that he has gone senile (even though he is only 46). And so now we are back to Chapter 2 and the end of the story (which happens in the beginning): Barbara decides that Billy can no longer care for himself and winds up taking control of his life and business so that he can rest in peace.

Booker's Seven Basic Plots Analysis: Rebirth

A Young Hero or Heroine Falls Under the Shadow of the Dark Power

Billy Pilgrim gets drafted to join the American army during World War II. He is sent to Europe, where the Germans capture him.

For a While, All May Seem to Go Reasonably Well

There is never a very strong sense that things are going well for Billy, even when he is back in New York State and successfully running his optometry business. Nevertheless, his initial captivity does not seem as threatening as it might, what with the British officers singing *The Pirates of Penzance* and Billy's assignment to work in an enriched syrup factory. He is a POW, but his position does not seem quite as dire as you might expect.

But It All Gets Worse

Sure, Billy can endure most of his captivity, but it's not all musical comedy and Brits performing *Cinderella*. As a captive of the German army, Billy has no control over his own fate, and as a

result, he has no way of influencing anything that happens to him, good or bad. Because of this total lack of control, Billy is forced to bear witness to the total destruction of the city of Dresden. This is the absolute worst thing that has or will ever happen to him, and it is utterly beyond his control.

This Continues For a Long Time
As Billy struggles with the aftermath of the war, even his literal freedom from German captivity and his return to upstate New York cannot free him from the unhappiness his war experience has left him with. Having lost control of his life as a POW, Billy is very slow to regain power over his own fate.

Miraculous Redemption
Oddly, Billy finally regains a sense of control over his own life by totally resigning himself to the fact that there *is* no free will. Once Billy totally gives himself over to the Tralfamadorian view that no individual can change a single moment in time, he is able to confront the misery he has been living with for so many years and put it aside. Of course, we have to ask whether Billy's refuge in Tralfamadore really represents a lasting answer to his personal sorrow, but for more on this, check out our "Three Act Plot Analysis."

Three Act Plot Analysis

Act I
For all of its circular logic and experimental writing, the set-up for *Slaughterhouse-Five* is actually quite simple: Billy Pilgrim, a young guy from upstate New York attending night classes in optometry, gets drafted and sent to Europe to fight in World War II. The Germans take him prisoner before he even has a chance to fire a single shot.

Act II
The second act is the part of the story where everything seems as far as possible from an ending, and Billy spends most of his time in this state of suspended action. Like a pawn in a chess game, he is constantly being moved here and there: by the Americans, who send him to war; by the Germans, who take him prisoner; by the Americans again, when they send him back to the States; and then by his family, who get him married and settle him down in his father-in-law's business. Billy seems to have very little say in his own life.

Act III
Act III is supposed to be the moment in a story when all of the plot's problems get resolved. But the issues that come up in *Slaughterhouse-Five* – how can Billy get over the pain of aging, death, and war? – do not really have solutions. However, Billy's personal problem of how to change his own really terrible experience of the world does have a temporary resolution, at least: his travels to Tralfamadore.

The Tralfamadorian belief that neither death nor pain has any meaning frees Billy from the suffering that his war experiences have caused him. This freedom may be short-lived, however. His daughter's total rejection of his Tralfamadorianism foreshadows potential future restrictions on his life – and perhaps even committal to an old-age home with his mother.

Study Questions

1. We here at Shmoop think that, factually speaking, Billy's trips to Tralfamadore are at least questionable and possibly outright hallucinations. Does it make a difference to your understanding of the philosophy of *Slaughterhouse-Five* if you read Billy's experiences on Tralfamadore literally as alien abductions? If *Slaughterhouse-Five* is a straight-up science-fiction novel, do we get the same lessons on fate and free will?
2. All of the women characters in this book (except Mary O'Hare) are either portrayed as dumb (Lily Rumfoord, Maggie White, and Valencia Pilgrim) or obnoxious (Barbara Pilgrim and Nancy the reporter). Are ladies getting short shrift here? Do the guys come off any better? And what makes Mary O'Hare so special?
3. There's the time travel and then there's the alien abduction. Billy comes unstuck in time in 1944 and is *then* abducted by aliens in 1967, he says. Why are these two separate events? What does the time travel do for Billy's character that the abduction doesn't?
4. *Slaughterhouse-Five* blurs the line between truth and fiction with the biographical details in Vonnegut's own life that keep creeping into the fictional parts of the story. A lot of other real people's words also make it into the novel. For example, there are quotes from poet Theodore Roethke (1.20.1) and the Gideon *Bible* (1.21.1). Why does Vonnegut quote so much? How do these quotes challenge our definition of *Slaughterhouse-Five* as a novel? Which chapters seem to quote the most, and why?
5. Vonnegut refers to the Vietnam War and the assassinations of Robert Kennedy and Martin Luther King, Jr. While the content of the novel clearly focuses on World War II, how is *Slaughterhouse-Five* also a book about America in the 1960s?

Characters

All Characters

Billy Pilgrim Character Analysis

Billy is the main character of *Slaughterhouse-Five*, but he's not exactly the *hero* of the book. Or rather, he doesn't have the heroic qualities usually associated with the main soldier in a story about wartime.

Billy is a funny-looking optometry student when he gets drafted to enter the military. He is sent to fight in Luxembourg against the Germans in the Battle of the Bulge and is promptly captured by a small group of German scouts. He manages get on nearly everyone's bad side by being so feckless and pathetic, with his constant nightmares and his weak body, but he does survive where a lot of others don't. He even manages to make it through one of the worst atrocities of the war, the Dresden firebombing.

Billy believes that in 1944 he became unstuck in time. One reason that he is so incredibly nervous and awkward all the time is that he never knows which part of his life he is going to be performing next: an eye exam on a kid who's just lost his father in Vietnam, a speech to the Lions Club, his honeymoon with his wife, his stay in a prison hospital in the British compound of a POW camp in Germany, or one of many other moments we're treated to in the book. Billy's zipping back and forth among different moments of his life gives us a plot-level reason to experience the novel in the "Tralfamadorian" way, as an apparently random series of moments without a definite beginning or end.

Has Billy *Really* Been Abducted?
There is plenty of evidence throughout the novel that Billy is suffering from Post-Traumatic Stress Disorder (PTSD). We know Billy gets nightmares, because when he falls asleep in the boxcar in Germany that's taking him to a POW camp, the other prisoners don't want to sleep next to him due to his whimpering and kicking. He startles easily: when he hears a siren going off in Chapter 3, Section 6, he jumps and worries that World War III is coming. And one of the most prominent symptoms of PTSD, the reliving of horrific past experiences, becomes *literal* in Billy's case as he travels in time. But while Billy's numbness and exhaustion all fit into official symptoms of PTSD, his travels to Tralfamadore are something else again.

Billy's section of the novel starts out with the revelation that he believes he was abducted by a bunch of short green aliens from the planet Tralfamadore in 1967 to be part of a zoo exhibit on their planet. He goes on the radio and writes letters to the local newspaper explaining the Tralfamadorian concept of time. The Tralfamadorians think that time does not go forward; instead, all points in time exist simultaneously. Nothing happens before or after anything else,

so we cannot change anything and we never die. Sure, there are moments when we are dead or unborn, but those moments exist *alongside* our own living experiences. Billy feels that this should comfort us Earthlings who are afraid of death.

We get lots of indications that this is not meant to be a straight sci-fi kind of story and that Billy's account of his own experiences is unreliable. He only starts telling everyone about his experiences on Tralfamadore *after* he breaks his head open in a plane accident in 1968. Incidentally, this is kind of like the real-life experiences of the French author Céline, which the narrator mentions in the first chapter, who experiences "noises in his head" (1.20.2) after a head injury.

Billy's story of abduction appears to be strongly influenced by other events in the novel, so much so that it could be happening entirely inside his head rather than as part of the "real" world of the novel. For instance, his story of his life in a zoo on Tralfamadore seems to mimic the plot of a Kilgore Trout novel he reads in Chapter 9, Section 26. He watches a porn flick featuring the woman he claims to have been placed in captivity with, Montana Wildhack, in Chapter 9, Section 30. And the prayer engraved on Montana Wildhack's locket appears framed on the wall of Billy's real-life optometry office. (Check out our "Symbols, Imagery, Allegory" for more on the significance of Montana's locket.)

Yet, even if Billy's ideas about Tralfamadore are imagined, they *do* point to something both he and the narrator desperately crave after the suffering they have experienced. Billy comments, and the narrator agrees, that he wants the following written on his tombstone: "Everything Was Beautiful, And Nothing Hurt" (5.51).

Only in the Tralfamadorian world can one cherry-pick the good moments from life to relive endlessly. The truth of the matter is that most human lives involve suffering. As a witness of terrible violence, Billy Pilgrim struggles more than most to find a way to *explain* how life can be so unfair and meaningless. Billy's trauma over the war is so severe that he has to *leave Earth* (either in his mind or for real) to find comfort after all the violence he has seen.

In the end, what matters more than the reality or unreality of Billy's life on Tralfamadore (and after all, he's a fictional character, so the whole question is kind of moot) is his desperate longing for new ways to explain human suffering. The old models of religion and patriotism don't seem to solve anything for him. (For more on this subject, check out our theme on "Fate and Free Will.")

Is Billy Pilgrim a Character?
Even though most of the novel is focused on Billy, and he appears in nearly every section of every chapter, he is not what Vonnegut/the narrator would call a "character." Nothing happens to him of his own choosing: he gets drafted into war; he goes along with his marriage to the unattractive but well-meaning Valencia Pilgrim; he gets bullied by his daughter, Barbara. He is just not an assertive guy.

There is a reason for this lack of action, which the narrator very helpfully explains. "There are almost no characters in this story," he says, "and almost no dramatic confrontations, because most of the people in it are so sick and so much the listless playthings of enormous forces" (8.4.1). Billy is too ill and weak to be an active character. Instead, he is forced to watch terrible things happen, things that are so awful that they send him out of time (either truly or in his own mind) to experience his own death many years before it happens (2.25.2).

The closest Billy comes to direct action is when he breaks out of the hospital to get on a radio talk show to spread the word about Tralfamadore. In other words, he becomes a "character" only after he goes crazy. And even then, it's to tell the world that he's been abducted *against his will* by aliens; he can't take credit for these ideas about life, the universe, and everything.

Billy Pilgrim Timeline and Summary

- Billy Pilgrim is an optometry school student in upstate New York when he is drafted to join the army in 1944.
- He is sent to Luxembourg to fight the Germans in the Battle of the Bulge.
- He gets lost behind enemy lines and falls in with a bullying eighteen-year old, Roland Weary.
- He becomes unstuck in time and starts jumping around to random moments in his life without warning.
- He gets taken prisoner and is sent to a POW compound just inside the German border. Weary dies of gangrene on the way.
- At the compound, Billy meets Paul Lazzaro and Edgar Derby. Lazzaro swears revenge on Billy for Weary's death.
- Billy and Edgar Derby are sent on to Dresden, Germany, to live in an abandoned slaughterhouse.
- Billy and Derby both survive the Dresden firestorm, but Derby is later executed for stealing a teapot from the ruins.
- After the war ends, Billy is sent home to upstate New York, where he finishes his optometry degree.
- He gets engaged to Valencia Merble and has a nervous breakdown.
- Billy recovers, marries Valencia, has two children (Robert and Barbara), and settles down to make lots of money in optometry.
- In 1968 Billy gets into a plane crash on his way to an optometry conference in Montreal.
- He has a terrible skull fracture. Valencia dies of carbon monoxide poisoning on her way to see him in the hospital.
- Billy recovers from the skull fracture and then runs away from the hospital.
- He goes to New York City to tell the world about the planet Tralfamadore, where he claims to have spent lots of time. This is possible without anyone noticing because he is a time

traveler.

- Billy tells the world that the Tralfamadorians believe that time does not move forward.
- Every individual moment in time happens at the exact same time as every other moment, so the past, the present, and the future are illusions.
- Also, because the future cannot possibly be changed, humans do not have free will. We should just sit back and accept that life is the way it is.
- Barbara Pilgrim, Billy's daughter, hears that he has been telling the world about his travels in a Tralfamadorian flying saucer.
- She feels that Billy has gone senile, so she threatens to put him in an old-age home along with his mother.

The Narrator Character Analysis

The narrator is pretty much Kurt Vonnegut. He talks from the first person perspective about the experience of writing this very novel, and he mentions lots of details about his own life that match Vonnegut's own biography.

So why don't we just call him Kurt Vonnegut? Well, first off, *he* doesn't call himself that in the book. And second, even if this guy is a stand-in for real-life Kurt Vonnegut, he is still a character within a fictional novel. There are lots of real details in the narrator's account of himself, but he is also a fictional device meant to tell a story.

The narrator is caught up in this contradiction: he was *at* the firebombing at Dresden (see "In a Nutshell"), he *saw* it, and yet, because it is so personally enormous to him, he cannot find the words to write about it.

The Narrator as a Pillar of Salt

The narrator compares himself to Lot's wife, the Biblical figure who was punished by God for turning back to look at the destruction of Sodom and Gomorrah in Genesis 19 (she was turned into a pillar of salt). Although he knows about the terrible things Germany did as a nation during World War II – a man at a party, for instance, tells him that the Germans "made soap and candles out of the fat of dead Jews" (1.6.6) – he still cannot help but feel pity and sorrow for the thousands of ordinary Germans killed in front of him during the war. He, like Lot's wife, even though it means that his book will be written be "a pillar of salt" (1.22.3).

The Narrator as a Comrade of Billy Pilgrim

The narrator keeps popping up throughout the "fictional" part of the novel revolving around Billy Pilgrim. When Billy first meets Wild Bob, the narrator comments that he and his war buddy, Bernard V. O'Hare, have both been to Wild Bob's hometown of Cody, Wyoming. When Billy stumbles into a latrine in the British POW compound in Chapter 5, one of the American soldiers with explosive diarrhea is the narrator himself. And when Billy arrives in Dresden and one of the

other POWs comments that the city looks like Oz, that's also the narrator.

We don't think there is one single answer for why the narrator keeps cropping up throughout the book as one of fictional Billy's real fellow prisoners. Maybe he's just trying to keep the reader's interest in Billy's adventures?

We think it might also be that Billy is a really *extreme* depiction of a clown in the middle of a war beyond his control. Some readers might start getting angry or offended at such an unflattering, unheroic depiction of the American soldier. (For more on this point, check out Mary O'Hare's "Character Analysis.") But the narrator himself really *was* in the war and really *did* get explosive diarrhea and really *did* think that Dresden was a lovely city, a lot like Oz. His experience of war was not romantic or heroic, which is what gives even this fictional novel its sense of real sadness and futility.

The Narrator Timeline and Summary

- The narrator talks about having been in World War II.
- He knew a guy who was shot for stealing a teapot, like Edgar Derby in the novel. He also knew a guy who threatened to have his enemies killed, like Paul Lazzaro.
- The narrator also witnesses the Dresden firestorm.
- He returns to the United States to study anthropology at the University of Chicago.
- After he finishes his degree, he becomes a journalist.
- He and his wife eventually move to Schenectady, New York, so that he can become a P.R. guy for General Electric.
- He starts planning his novel about Dresden by writing to the Air Force, which won't release any information to him because the raid is still top secret.
- Many years go by and the narrator becomes more successful. He has kids and makes money.
- The narrator finally signs a book contract with Seymour Lawrence to write three novels, one of which will be about Dresden.
- He goes to visit his old war buddy, Bernard O'Hare, so they can think up some stories about the war for him to write about.
- While he's visiting, Bernard's wife Mary tells the author not to write a book celebrating war.
- He promises Mary he will not: the narrator is going to write an anti-war book called *The Children's Crusade* .
- The narrator and Bernard O'Hare travel together to East Germany to look at the slaughterhouse where they stayed as prisoners of war.
- While there, they are driven in a taxi by a German veteran whose family died at Dresden. This guy's name is Gerhard Müller.
- The narrator dedicates *Slaughterhouse-Five* to Mary O'Hare and Gerhard Müller.

- And he publishes this very book.

Kilgore Trout Character Analysis

Kilgore Trout is a (fictional) science fiction author whose stories bear a *significant resemblance* to Billy's descriptions of Tralfamadore. Trout writes many, many books, but no one besides Billy and Eliot Rosewater, another veteran, have ever heard of him. The thing is, he has great ideas, but he's a terrible writer.

The most important thing about Trout is that he imagines the world operating by new and different rules, in ways that Billy finds comforting and necessary after being so disappointed by reality during the war.

Trout lives in Billy's hometown and the two become acquainted. When we actually meet Trout as a character we find that he is socially maladjusted and sadistic. At the same time, he has greater insight into Billy than any of the other characters. When Billy has a flashback to the aftermath of Dresden while watching a barbershop perform at his anniversary party, it is Trout who suggests that Billy has seen through a *time window* (8.16.4). Given that Billy sees himself as a time traveler, this is pretty perceptive, but it is also an imaginative way of describing a flashback, a moment when you are suddenly looking back at a terrible event from your own past.

Maybe Trout is yet another stand-in for Vonnegut himself: after all, Trout *is* a writer, and he *does* invent a lot of the concepts that come up in the novel. What's more, Vonnegut also reinvents the universe to fit new rules – *Slaughterhouse-Five* and many of his other novels have fit into the category of science fiction. Which would make Rosewater's comment that Trout has great ideas but is a terrible writer kind of an in-joke or self-jab on Vonnegut's part.

The Works of Kilgore Trout

(1) *Maniacs in the Fourth Dimension* (Chapter 5, Section 25)

Kilgore Trout claims that there really are vampires and werewolves, heaven and hell, but we just can't see them, since they're in the fourth dimension.

(2) *The Gospel of Outer Space* (Chapter 5, Section 30)

The hero of this novel is an alien (who looks like a Tralfamadorian) who wants to know how Christians can be so cruel. The alien decides that the problem is the New Testament, which is supposed to teach people to be merciful but actually seems to teach them: "Before you kill somebody, make absolutely sure he isn't well connected" (5.30.7). The problem is that the man the Romans crucify is already the son of God, so *of course* everyone's going to think it's wrong to kill him.

If Christ were just a nobody, would it have been any more OK to kill him? The alien decides it would be better if Christ were not actually the son of God, but still said all the same stuff. Then God could come down just before Christ dies on the cross to say that he is *adopting* Christ, and that from that day on, it is wrong to persecute anyone who torments "a bum who has no connections" (5.32.3)

(3) The money tree (Chapter 8, Section 7)
Trout describes a money tree with twenty-dollar bills for leaves that attracts people to it so they will kill each other around the tree's base and become its fertilizer.

(4) *The Gutless Wonder* (Chapter 8, Section 8)
Even though this book is written long before World War II, it still predicts the dropping of jellied petroleum devices to cause firestorms. The person who drops these special bombs is actually a robot. He is shunned by society not because he is a mass murderer, but because he has bad breath. Once he fixes his breath, everyone welcomes him.

(5) The mysterious zoo novel (Chapter 8, Section 26)
This novel is sitting in the porn shop where Billy sees the film of Montana Wildhack before going on the radio to talk about Tralfamadore. The novel is about a man and a woman from Earth who are kidnapped by aliens and put in a zoo.

(6) The mysterious Jesus time-traveling novel (Chapter 8, Section 28)
This is another porn shop Kilgore Trout novel. The hero travels back in time to find out whether Jesus really died on the cross, or if he was taken down before his death, thus explaining the "Resurrection." The time traveler arrives before Jesus has discovered that he is the son of God, while he is still working as a carpenter for Joseph, and Jesus builds an execution device at the order of the Romans. But then Jesus himself is crucified and the time traveler finds out that his heart has really stopped beating: he is absolutely dead.

(7) *The Big Board* (Chapter 10, Section 3)
The narrator seems to imply that Trout gets the idea for this novel from Billy, who says that the Tralfamadorians really like Charles Darwin. The reason is that he tells us that death of the weakest improves the species. Trout uses this idea in *The Big Board*, in which aliens ask the hero about Darwin and golf.

When you look at all of Trout's works together like this, you can see *a lot* of the elements of Billy's own life story in them: the Tralfamadorians in *The Gospel of Outer Space*; the ethical and religious issues in *The Gospel of Outer Space*, *The Gutless Wonder*, and the time-traveling novel of Chapter 8; the alien zoo in the mysterious zoo novel of Chapter 8; and the fourth dimension in *Maniacs in the Fourth Dimension*. This makes us wonder, once again, if Billy is meant to be crazy in the novel – or whether it even matters. After all, both Billy and Trout are *both* fictional creations of Kurt Vonnegut, so who cares which of them gives ideas to the other? *Neither* of them is real. Whoa, our heads are spinning.

The Tralfamadorians Character Analysis

The Tralfamadorians are the aliens who bring Billy to their planet to exhibit him in a zoo. They also kidnap a twenty-year-old actress/porn star named Montana Wildhack so that the two can mate. The Tralfamadorians are green and shaped like toilet plungers, with hands at the end of their long, stick-like bodies.

In many ways, the Tralfamadorians are subtly compared to the Germans. The first thing the Germans do when Billy arrives at their prison camp is to make him take off his clothes, which is also the first thing the Tralfamadorians do when Billy arrives on their planet. When a German prison guard punches an American in the face and the American asks why, the German answers, "Vy you? Vy anybody?" (5.9.4). Similarly, the Tralfamadorians refuse to consider the question "why" they abducted Billy: they say, "There is no *why*" (4.7.6).

But most important, the Tralfamadorians, like the Germans, totally remove Billy's *choices*: they take him captive and there is nothing Billy can do about it. He is forced to live (he believes) in a geodesic dome on Tralfamadore just as he is forced to live in a slaughterhouse in Dresden.

The lessons the Tralfamadorians teach Billy about time (about which, see Billy's "Character Analysis") are kind of a mixed blessing. It comforts Billy to think that time is totally predetermined and unchangeable and there is no free will. This Tralfamadorian faith in the total pointlessness of trying to change anything makes Billy feel like everything he has gone through, no matter how awful, *could not* have gone any other way.

At the same time, we have to wonder if it isn't kind of messed up that Billy's idea of Tralfamadorian philosophy frees him from taking any blame or responsibility for his own actions. Billy embraces the thinking of Tralfamadore because it absolves him from even *trying* to change the way things are. He doesn't prevent his son from going to war, he doesn't attempt to remind people of the bombing of Dresden – nothing. What Billy actively chooses to do is to soothe the world with the news of Tralfamadore – to tell the world that it's OK that he has suffered horribly and will die eventually, when suffering should *never* be OK.

The narrator of the story resolves that he has to write about Dresden and the war, even if trying to stop war may as well be like trying to stop glaciers (1.2.12). In a sense, maybe the act of writing *Slaughterhouse-Five* is a way of writing against the powerlessness and sorrow that World War II, the Germans, the Tralfamadorians, and even death itself seem to inspire in him. For more on this topic, see our theme on "Fate and Free Will."

Edgar Derby Character Analysis

Edgar Derby is the unfortunate high school teacher and slightly older-than-average soldier who winds up getting shot at the end of the war for stealing a teapot from the rubble of Dresden. He is tried and executed by a German firing squad, and Billy is among the group of POWs who have to dig his grave. The narrator comments on the dramatic irony of the situation: Edgar survives the misery of the firebombing of Dresden only to be executed for a trivial "crime" (1.3.19).

During the war, though, Derby is one of the most idealistic characters of the bunch: he winds up being elected head of the American group of POWs, and he also tells off creepy American Nazi Howard W. Campbell, Jr. Derby dreams of the letters he would write to his wife if he could, telling her that he is safe. He seems like a nice guy, but that's not enough to save his life.

Paul Lazzaro Character Analysis

Paul Lazzaro is the fake name of a real guy the narrator mentions in the first chapter, who "really *did* threaten to have his personal enemies killed by hired gunmen after the war" (1.1.1). Lazzaro is a fellow American POW with a grudge against Billy because he believes it's his fault that Roland Weary dies of gangrene.

Of course, Lazzaro had not known Weary before meeting him on the train from Luxembourg to Germany where Weary dies. Lazzaro's insane, murderous loyalty to Weary's memory doesn't really have anything to do with Weary. Lazzaro is a guy with a permanent chip on his shoulder, a total psychopath who judges every encounter he has with a person based on how much respect they show him. Revenge is the sweetest thing in life for Lazzaro, and he is always looking for an excuse to get some. The narrator compares Lazzaro to a rabid dog (6.9.3)

Lazzaro's threats seem to work, because Billy really does believe that he is going to succeed in shooting him out of the blue. That is how Billy sees himself dying, and he has even seen the date: February 13, 1976. We cannot help but notice that February 13, the date of Billy's projected death, is the same day as the Dresden firebombing. We're just sayin'.

Anyway, there is no way to prevent or change this future assassination. Remember, according to the Tralfamadorians, we have no free will. Check out the Tralfamadorians' "Character Analysis" and our theme on "Fate and Free Will" for more on this point.

Roland Weary Character Analysis

Roland Weary is an unpleasant little turd who finds Billy wandering around behind enemy lines

after the Battle of the Bulge in Luxembourg. He is an eighteen-year-old American bully who thinks it's cool that his father collects medieval torture implements. Weary is incredibly well-equipped with everything you could possibly need for war – good boots, sharp implements, lots of weapons – and he likes to fantasize about what a great soldier he is. In reality, he's a violent little creep who fires one shot during his first battle, which alerts the Germans to where his machine gun is. As a result, the Germans kill Weary's entire gunner detail.

Weary won't leave Billy behind, *not* because he likes Billy or is compassionate or anything. Instead, Weary is busy creating a story in his head about the war. In it, he and two other scouts manage to drag Billy to safety even though Billy is totally unequipped for battle. Weary calls his trio "The Three Musketeers." As he drags Billy across the Luxembourg countryside, he fantasizes so hard about how he and these scouts will be decorated with medals for saving Billy that he completely loses track of where he is.

When the two scouts lose patience and leave Weary and Billy behind, Weary blames Billy. When the Germans come, Weary is pointing his gun at Billy. The Germans cannot understand why one American would be trying to shoot another on German territory. (This irony of pointless violence in the midst of much larger historical events repeats itself with Paul Lazzaro, by the way.)

Weary winds up dying of gangrene because his feet are too damaged by a pair of wooden clogs the Germans make him wear in exchange for his own state-of-the-art combat boots. He dies cursing Billy's name. Weary is as inexperienced as Billy himself, but he has grand ideals about war and its glories. He believes in and thrives on violence, thus making an already awful situation even worse for everyone around him.

Valencia Pilgrim Character Analysis

Valencia is Billy's extremely large but very good-natured wife. She never thought anyone would marry her because of her size, so she bursts into tears with gratitude the night of their honeymoon. She loves Billy so much that, when she hears he has been in a plane crash, she drives to the hospital with her eyes so full of tears that she can't see the road. She winds up having a car accident that leaves her vehicle so damaged that she dies of carbon monoxide poisoning.

Like Billy, Valencia has her own ways of coping with the disappointing realities of life. When Billy is making love to her the night of her honeymoon, she imagines that he is Christopher Columbus and she is Queen Elizabeth I of England (never mind that they weren't even alive at the same time). It's this kind of active fantasy life that leads her to ask Billy to tell her about the war. She thinks the details of his fighting life will be hot. But Billy doesn't really seem to want to tell her anything. They share lives, but neither of them is passionate or smart enough to talk about the things that really matter to them.

Barbara Pilgrim Character Analysis

Barbara is Billy's daughter. In 1968, when Billy writes his letters about Tralfamadore to the local newspaper, she is only twenty-one and her mother has just died of carbon monoxide poisoning. The loss of her mother, Billy's very public alien abduction stories, and her sudden responsibility (along with her husband) for all of Billy's businesses turns Barbara into, in the words of the narrator, a "bitchy flibbertigibbet" (2.9.3). She really is worried about Billy, but she's also incredibly disrespectful – she insists on taking over his life, making him even more powerless than he has been throughout the rest of the novel.

Robert Pilgrim Character Analysis

Robert is Billy's son. He is a wild kid in high school, but then he joins the Marines and straightens out. In 1968 Robert is deployed in Vietnam, but he flies home when he receives the news of Billy's plane crash and Valencia's death by carbon monoxide.

Robert doesn't have much of a character. Billy even thinks to himself that he doesn't really know Robert, if there even is much to know (8.20.2). The most significant thing about Robert is that he is a Green Beret in the Marine Corps (made famous, in part, by the movie *The Green Berets* starring the John Wayne that Mary O'Hare is so concerned about). Robert seems to fit that perfect army profile the way Billy didn't: rough kid who makes good serving in the military. At the same time, there is a weird disconnect between the generations. Even though Billy has been totally screwed up by his war experiences, he's happy that his own son is in the army.

This is one point where Billy and the narrator really differ. The narrator tells his sons that they are "under no circumstances to take part in massacres, and that news of massacres of enemies is not to fill them with satisfaction or glee" (1.16.1). Even though war has thoroughly messed Billy up, he isn't assertive or reflective enough to condemn it, or to dissuade his own son from involvement in a war that, by 1969, had come under criticism for its huge number of civilian deaths.

Billy's Father Character Analysis

We don't get to see much of Billy's father. We know pretty much four things about him: (1) He is a barber. That's why Billy's mother is so proud when Billy finishes optometry school and marries the boss's daughter; it's an economic move up for the Pilgrim family. (2) He throws Billy into the deep end of the YMCA pool to teach him how to swim, and Billy almost drowns. When he comes unstuck in time for the first time, in 1944, this is the moment he travels to, when

he first seems to experience death. (3) Billy's father also freaks Billy out by taking him to the edge of the Grand Canyon and making him look down. And (4), Billy's father dies in a hunting accident while Billy is on maneuvers in the army.

All of this throwing-Billy-into-the-deep-end stuff makes us think that Billy's dad is supposed to be more of a manly man than Billy (though that isn't exactly a high hurdle). Billy has not learned much from his father in any obvious ways – unlike Roland Weary, who inherits all of his cruelty from his father. The narrator's dad seems somewhat in-between these two. Like Billy's dad, he a hunting enthusiast, but he is also a kind man. The narrator can take what his father has left him, his gun collection, and put it aside while understanding and respecting what it meant to his father.

Billy's Mother Character Analysis

Billy's mother is rather like his wife, Valencia – Freud would have a field day. She is incredibly insensitive and barely notices what's going on with Billy at any given time. When Billy is staying at the veteran's hospital after his mental breakdown, he cannot bear to talk to her because he feels guilty that, after all the trouble she went through to give birth to him, he doesn't even like life. Instead of trying to talk to Billy or to understand his troubles, she carries on a conversation with the man in the next bed. She discusses really personal things: Billy's business future, his upcoming marriage to Valencia, and all the day-to-day stuff in his life that he cannot handle any more.

The one time we see Billy's mother stop talking and gain some awareness is when she is ill with pneumonia in 1965, when Billy is forty-one. She looks around and asks, "How did I get so *old*?" (2.26.6). Her entire life has changed and she wasn't even paying attention.

Howard W. Campbell, Jr. Character Analysis

Howard W. Campbell, Jr., like Bertram Copeland Rumfoord, actually appeared in a previous Vonnegut novel, called *Mother Night* (1961). Like Roland Weary, Campbell has this odd invented identity for himself, a bizarre mix of Nazi and American Cowboy. He is a traitor to the U.S. who has joined the German army and written essays about American soldiers and their behavior in German captivity. We also find out that he hangs himself at the end of the war. Campbell believes that American soldiers make disgusting prisoners because they have no self-respect: they come from a country that hates the poor, and, as they themselves are often poor, they hate themselves.

While Campbell is an obvious whacko, with his spurs and swastikas, he does make some relevant points about American poverty in Chapter 5, Sections 55-8. Like all the potential villains in this novel, Campbell is more than just evil. He truly seems to feel principled outrage at the

common assumption Americans make that if they are smart, they should be rich, and if they are not rich, it's a personal failing.

Bertram Copeland Rumfoord Character Analysis

Bertram Copeland Rumfoord, originally appearing in another of Vonnegut's books, *The Sirens of Titan* (1959), is an incredibly energetic 70-year-old with a hot 23-year old wife. He winds up breaking a leg in a skiing accident in Vermont at the same time that Billy has his plane crash. The two share a hospital room. Rumfoord is working on a short history of the U.S. Air Force, and he is particularly interested in researching the raid on Dresden. But he cannot believe that Billy was actually there because he is so certain Billy is a useless waste of space, a vegetable who is just repeating words he hears Rumfoord saying.

The thing about Rumfoord is that he is a kind of superman: an athletic, respected Harvard professor who cannot believe that anyone as pathetic as Billy could have anything to contribute to the world. Rumfoord eventually decides that Billy *was* probably at Dresden, but he is not interested in talking to him about his experiences. Instead, he insists on repeating over and over that the firebombing was necessary, even though Billy has never said that it wasn't. Rumfoord is paranoid about bleeding hearts pretending that the Air Force might have done the wrong thing by causing so many civilian deaths. He wants to celebrate the Dresden firebombing as "a howling success" (9.10.5).

Bernard V. O'Hare Character Analysis

Bernard V. O'Hare is the narrator's war buddy who accompanies him on his trip back to the slaughterhouse where they took shelter from the Dresden firebombing. He seems to be in the story pretty much as a support to the narrator's own thought processes – a sounding board.

It is in interaction with O'Hare that the narrator encounters (a) the guy's wife, Mary, to whom the novel is dedicated; (b) *Extraordinary Popular Delusions and the Madness of Crowds*, which tells the narrator about the Children's Crusade; (c) *Dresden, History, Stage and Gallery*, which describes not only the city pre-World War II, but also a previous bombing siege Dresden underwent in 1760; and (d) some key facts about world population and human dignity at the end of the novel.

Mary O'Hare Character Analysis

Mary O'Hare is the wife of the narrator's war buddy, Bernard V. O'Hare. She is initially furious with the narrator because she thinks this great Dresden book he's writing is going to be a

celebration of war and of his own experiences as a POW. She thinks that the more attractive writers and filmmakers make war seem, the more stupid wars we're going to have. The narrator promises her he will call the book *The Children's Crusade* . (Check out "What's Up With the Title?" for more on this). Mary O'Hare is also one of the two characters (along with Gerhard Müller) to whom the narrator dedicates the book, presumably in recognition of her passionately anti-war feelings.

A side note: Mary O'Hare is also a nurse, which the narrator calls "a lovely thing for a woman to be" (1.10.1). In general, the narrator seems to have only good things to say about the medical profession, which he contrasts pretty obviously with the whole army apparatus he is writing against.

Probably the strongest example of this medicine-life/army-death opposition happens when Billy Pilgrim is in the hospital with a fractured skull and Bertram Copeland Rumfoord keeps telling his wife that the doctors should just pull the plug because Billy is a waste of space. The doctors refuse because they are "devoted to the idea that weak people should be helped as much as possible, that nobody should die" (9.14.3). For more on Rumfoord as an extreme example of pro-army feeling, check out his "Character Analysis."

Gerhard Müller Character Analysis

The second person who appears in the book's dedication after Mary O'Hare is Gerhard Müller, the German taxi driver who takes the narrator and Bernard V. O'Hare to the real-life slaughterhouse where they took shelter from the Dresden firestorm. Müller's life is like some kind of weird reflection of the narrator's own: he was a prisoner of war of the Americans during the war, and his mother burned to death in the Dresden firebombing.

The narrator particularly likes Müller because he sends O'Hare a Christmas card hoping that they will meet again "if the accident will" (1.1.5). This awkward phrase really emphasizes one of the main themes of the book: chance. So much of the book is made up of Deep Thoughts on free will and fate, and Gerhard Müller's accidental meeting with the narrator in his taxicab is only one example. Check out our "Fate and Free Will" theme section for more on this point.

The Narrator's Dad Character Analysis

The narrator's father only appears twice in the novel, but each time he seems to be fairly revealing of the narrator's own character. First, in Chapter 1, Section 4, when his father points out to the narrator that none of his books seem to have villains, the narrator answers that the war taught him not to cast anyone as a villain. This seems consistent with the narrator's overall point that Dresden's miseries are worth writing about *even if* Germany did terrible things during the war. After all, human suffering is human suffering.

The second place the narrator's father appears is in Chapter 10, Section 1, where the narrator tells us that he was a nice man with a gun collection, which he passed on to the narrator. The narrator never uses the guns, though; he had seen too much senseless violence in the war.

The Narrator's Wife Character Analysis

The narrator's wife is pretty darn minor as a character, but never let it be said that we here at Shmoop aren't thorough! Like Bernard V. O'Hare, she appears to be mostly a sounding board for the narrator. He tells her that he has written to the Air Force asking for information about Dresden, only to be told that the Dresden raid has been classified. While the narrator is working out how to write about something so horrible that it is beyond words, he keeps explaining different aspects of his project to the people in his life to try to get his own handle on what he wants to say.

Montana Wildhack Character Analysis

Montana Wildhack is a hot twenty-year-old actress whom the Tralfamadorians pair Billy with in their zoo. After a gentlemanly week of waiting, Billy has sex with her and the two conceive a baby. While Billy is in New York trying to tell the world about time and Tralfamadore, he imagines Montana back in the zoo nursing their six-month-old baby. Montana appears to be a complete fantasy for Billy, a totally understanding and attractive woman who demands no real strings.

Eliot Rosewater Character Analysis

Eliot Rosewater is a captain in World War II. He winds up in the same veteran's hospital Billy checks himself into when he has his nervous breakdown before marrying Valencia. They both have had terrible experiences during the war which have left them not enjoying life very much. Rosewater also has a serious drinking problem. He finds it necessary to read a lot of science fiction, in which authors try to reinvent the universe. He introduces Billy to sci-fi, specifically the works of author Kilgore Trout.

Wild Bob Character Analysis

Wild Bob is an American colonel and prisoner along with Billy at the Luxembourg/German border. As he is extremely sick, he imagines that Billy is a member of his own regiment and gives him a very moving speech. Wild Bob tells Billy that, if he's ever in Cody, Wyoming, to

"just ask for Wild Bob!" (3.25.5). The narrator refers several times to this line throughout the novel. Both the narrator and Bernard V. O'Hare have been to Cody, Wyoming, though whether this means Wild Bob was a real man Vonnegut knew, we cannot say.

There is something tragic about the pointlessness of Wild Bob speaking his dying words to a boy who's not even in his regiment. His death corresponds to the novel's general sense that the big issues of World War II – Nazis, anti-Semitism, fascism – have totally passed certain soldiers by. Instead, they are caught up in their own individual fantasies of who they are and what their lives mean, right up until the moment of their death.

The Englishmen Character Analysis

The Englishmen are the first group of POWs the Americans meet when they are shipped from Luxembourg to a temporary prisoner camp in Germany. The Englishmen were captured early in the war and have been using their time to exercise and entertain themselves with light opera. (Seriously: they're singing *The Pirates of Penzance* to welcome the Americans when they arrive at the compound.) These English soldiers are incredibly healthy, well-trained and all-around awesome. Because they look like every stereotype of an Englishman you could imagine, the Germans love them. The Englishmen seem mostly to be foils (contrasts) of the American soldiers, who in comparison are ill-fed, undertrained, exhausted, and unprepared for war.

The British Colonel Character Analysis

The British colonel is the head of the Englishmen in the POW compound Billy stops at before heading to Dresden. He is incredibly committed to hygiene and believes that once you lose interest in your appearance, you're done for. Of course Billy has never been interested in his appearance – in fact, he looks incredibly clownish and ridiculous – and yet he still manages to survive the war.

What's important about the British colonel, and the Englishmen in general, is that they still have these intense ideals about being officers and gentlemen. But they can afford to have these dreams – after all, they have spent most of the war out of commission, eating, exercising, and not having to fight. It is one of the great ironies of the book that the guys who most want to fight can't and the ones who least want to – like Billy – get sent out to witness massacres like those at Dresden.

Lionel Merble Character Analysis

Lionel Merble is Valencia Pilgrim's father and Billy's father-in-law. He is an optometrist who brings Billy in on his business, giving him the kind of wealth and opportunity Billy never had growing up. It's on a trip to an optometry conference with Lionel that Billy has the plain crash that fractures his skull and puts him in the hospital with Bertram Copeland Rumfoord. Lionel is killed instantly.

Lionel's only real significance in the book is his liking for barbershop quartets. He listens to one perform on the flight that kills him, the same quartet that sang at Billy's wedding anniversary party in Chapter 8. This barbershop quartet makes Billy feel sick and unsettled because the four open-mouthed men remind him of his four German guards in Dresden.

Nanny Character Analysis

Nanny is the narrator's daughter. It's on a trip with her to the New York World's Fair in 1964 that the narrator first meets up with Bernard V. O'Hare to talk over the war.

Nancy Character Analysis

Nancy is a very minor character indeed, since she only appears in the fifth section of the first chapter, but she is one of several examples (including Bernard Copeland Rumfoord) of characters who are really hardened and unsympathetic to the suffering of others. She doesn't hurt anyone directly, but she hears about a man being squashed by a falling elevator and insists that the narrator break the news to the man's wife to get her reaction directly. She asks the narrator if seeing this guy's squashed body has bothered him, and the narrator answers, "Heck, no, Nancy . . . I've seen lots worse than that in the war" (1.5.14). This kind of purposeless emotional cruelty is precisely what the novel seeks to avoid by humanizing all of its characters.

The Blue Fairy Godmother Character Analysis

Paul Lazzaro tries to steal a pack of cigarettes from under the pillow of an Englishman, who wakes up and breaks his arm. This Englishman played the role of Blue Fairy Godmother in the English officers' production of *Cinderella* for the Americans during their first night in the POW camp. Lazzaro promises that he will have the Blue Fairy Godmother killed after the war for daring to break his arm, but the Godmother (who actually seems kind of menacing) says that he'll get Lazzaro before that happens. It's this guy who provokes Lazzaro into telling Edgar Derby and Billy Pilgrim his whole philosophy on revenge (see Paul Lazzaro's "Character Analysis").

The German Major Character Analysis

The head of the POW camp where Billy Pilgrim meets the English officers. The German major loves the English prisoners because they look like what soldiers *should* look like. Conversely, he is disgusted by the Americans, who are all in poor physical shape. He apologizes to the British colonel for having to put up with these Americans and promises that they will be sent further east into Germany soon.

Werner Gluck Character Analysis

Werner is a sixteen-year-old German charged with guarding Billy and Edgar Derby when they first arrive at Slaughterhouse-Five in Dresden. He does not know his way around, and as he tries to find the kitchen he accidentally leads them into a communal shower where some German refugee girls from the Eastern Front are bathing. This accident is the first time Billy sees a naked woman.

Maggie White Character Analysis

Maggie White is the wife of an optometrist and a guest at Billy's anniversary party, to which he has invited Kilgore Trout. Trout is a hit with the optometrists because they all think he is some kind of big successful type. Maggie is not too bright, but she's beautiful, and Trout chats her up with lies about his books and their plots.

Lily Rumfoord Character Analysis

Lily Rumfoord is, along with Maggie White is a hot but dumb woman who attaches herself to a powerful man. She is the 23-year old wife of 70-year-old Bertram Copeland Rumfoord. She brings him books for his work but barely knows how to read herself.

The Maori Character Analysis

The Maori are a group of native people from New Zealand. When Billy is assigned to dig up bodies in the rubble of Dresden, he works with a Maori man who was captured in the North African battle of Tobruk. When the Maori goes down into one of the pits with human remains in it, the smell is so overwhelming that he cannot stop vomiting and eventually dies of the dry heaves.

The Dogs Character Analysis

There are a bunch of dogs in this novel. There is Sandy, the narrator's dog; Spot, a (sadly deceased) dog of Billy's; and Princess, the freezing cold German shepherd who accompanies the soldiers that capture Billy and Roland Weary in the cold forests of Luxembourg.

These dogs appear briefly, and we don't want to read too much into this, but it does seem significant that when Billy is on the run from the Germans in Luxembourg, he sometimes hears dogs barking. They indicate that the German troops are nearby and sound terrifying. But up close, all the dogs we meet in the book are loyal and likable. Even Princess, an imposing German shepherd, is just a frightened animal, cold and unfamiliar with war. This may sound like kind of an obvious message, but it remains true that appearances can be deceiving

Lance Rumfoord Character Analysis

Bertram Copeland Rumfoord's nephew, whom Billy Pilgrim happens to see from the window of his honeymoon suite long before he meets Bertram Copeland Rumfoord.

Cynthia Landry Character Analysis

Lance Rumfoord's wife.

Character Roles

Protagonist
Billy Pilgrim
The largely fictional part of *Slaughterhouse-Five* starts with the line: "Listen: Billy Pilgrim has come unstuck in time" (2.1.1). And from there on out, Billy's story dominates the novel: the narrative of his wartime troubles, his witnessing of the Dresden massacre, his return to the United States, and his decades-long struggle to deal with the aftermath of World War II provide the primary material of the book. While Billy is not the world's most forceful character, and we may not be left with a strong sense of who he really is as a person (about which, check out our "Character Analysis"), he is certainly the central focus of *Slaughterhouse-Five*.

Protagonist
The Narrator (Kurt Vonnegut)

As we have remarked in our sections on "Symbols, Imagery, Allegory," *Slaughterhouse-Five* constantly draws attention to the fact that it is a novel, and that narrator is using the characters to tell the story of his experience in Dresden. Given all the biographical detail and reflections on how we, as human beings, can cope with pain and death, we have to cite the narrator – and the author himself – as the alternate main character of the book. *Slaughterhouse-Five* is like a puppet-show where we can see both the puppet – Billy Pilgrim – and the puppeteer – Kurt Vonnegut. If Billy is just a puppet, then that makes Kurt Vonnegut our protagonist.

Antagonist
Roland Weary
Weary is a sad bully who attempts to beat up Billy Pilgrim while they are both on the wrong side of enemy lines. His nasty obsession with torture devices marks how deluded he is about the realities of war. He thinks all of these instruments of pain and death (like his three-cornered knife or the Iron Maiden of Nuremberg are neat tricks. But when he is actually on a battlefield, all he can do is fantasize about what kinds of heroic stories he'll tell his family when he gets back from the war. His blindness to the realities of the violence around him leaves him exposed to capture by the Germans. Weary's fantasy life is so extreme that he imagines that it is Billy who is responsible for his eventual death by gangrene. Even as he is dying, he can't let go of his stupid, petty resentments.

Antagonist
Paul Lazzaro
Paul Lazzaro spends the book in the middle of the most awful situation a soldier can find himself in: as a prisoner of war at a time when there is no food and nowhere to house enemy soldiers. And Paul Lazzaro, like Roland Weary before him, takes this awful situation and makes it ten times worse for his fellow captives. He constantly threatens violence, promising everyone he has a grudge against that he is going to have him killed after the war. He dreams of revenge and raping women. Even though Lazzaro has no power to carry out any of these terrible threats, the fact that he can sit in a war zone and want to see *more* death and *more* suffering is a mark of how crazy people can get. It makes sense that, out of all of the POWs in the novel, it would be Lazzaro who promises to kill Billy in revenge for Weary's death. Both Lazzaro and Weary represent the kind of bullying, stupid guys that war seems to bring out of the woodwork.

Antagonist
Bertram Copeland Rumfoord
Bertram Copeland Rumfoord is the opposite of Billy Pilgrim in every way: he's this incredibly healthy and athletic 70-year-old who was born rich and is married to a hot, young wife. Rumfoord looks at Billy and sees a pathetic weakling who deserves to die. If Weary and Lazzaro are the kind of guys who make wartime violence so bad *on* the battlefield, Rumfoord is kind who makes this violence possible from *off* the battlefield.

Rumfoord believes that might makes right, that stronger armies should make their enemies suffer, and that Dresden was an incredibly successful air raid that should be celebrated. His

planned history of the Air Force, in which he wants to glorify the Dresden firebombing, is the kind of book that makes war seem reasonable and positive. Guys like Rumfoord help popularize and glorify war– and in an anti-war book, that makes him an absolute villain.

Foils

The Narrator and Billy Pilgrim

We get into the relationship between the narrator and Billy Pilgrim in the narrator's "Character Analysis." Check it out!

Character Clues

Direct Characterization

Most of Billy Pilgrim's adventures are told in third person and without direct interference from the first-person narrator who starts and ends the book. At the same time, the narrator often tells us what to think of the people around Billy; the descriptions of the characters we get are pretty explicit and straightforward. We can find an example of this kind of direct characterization in the book's many descriptions of Roland Weary:

Billy and the scouts were skinny people. Roland Weary had fat to burn. . . . He had so much energy that he bustled back and forth between Billy and the scouts, delivering dumb messages which nobody had sent and which nobody was pleased to receive. He also began to suspect, since he was so much busier than anybody else, that he was the leader.

He was so hot and bundled up, in fact, that he had no sense of danger. . . . He was so snug in there that he was able to pretend he was safe at home, having survived the war, and that he was telling his parents and his sister a true war story – whereas the true war story was still going on. (2.24.1-2)

There is a lot of characterization going on in this passage. The contrast between Billy as skinny and Weary as fat seems to imply that Billy is vulnerable where Weary is spoiled. And Weary's layers of clothing show that he is (or at least, imagines himself to be) protected from the messed-up situation that he and Billy find themselves in.

The narrator also tells us directly that Weary "suspect[s] . . . that he is the leader" (though he clearly is not or should not be), that he has "no sense of danger," and that he is caught up in fantasies of what war is like because he is so good at ignoring the realities around him. There are plenty of physical descriptions of Weary, but the real sense we get of his character comes from the narrator's outright judgment of him as a human being. The narrator calls Weary "stupid and fat and mean" (2.17.1), and it doesn't get more direct than that.

Actions

Let's look at the same passage we talked about above, in "Direct Characterization." It's true

that the narrator is pretty direct about telling us what to think about Weary ("dumb" leaps to mind). At the same time, these descriptions of Weary do not exist in a vacuum. The narrator is not satisfied with *telling* us that Weary is "stupid and fat and mean" (2.17.1); he also has to *show* us that Weary is all of these things, through Weary's actions.

Weary runs back and forth between the scouts and Billy for no reason except to pretend that he is the leader of their group. He makes up stories about the war because he has no patience to look around him and see what is actually going on. These actions are definitely those of a "stupid" man; as for "mean," it doesn't get much crueler than beating up a fellow American soldier behind enemy lines, as Weary does in Chapter 2, Section 34.

Thoughts and Opinions

This is a novel about fate, free will, and human suffering, so we probably shouldn't be surprised that characters have strong opinions about one or all of these things. Take, for example, Bertram Copeland Rumfoord, Billy's roommate in the Vermont hospital where Billy recovers from his skull fracture:

It was difficult for Rumfoord to take Billy seriously, since Rumfoord had so long considered Billy a repulsive non-person who would be much better off dead. (9.12.1)

We have spent the whole novel learning what Billy has gone through and how strong the narrator's regard is for the value of human life. Then along comes Rumfoord, who takes Billy's physical weakness as a sign that he is worth nothing, that he is a vegetable who should be killed for his own good. Rumfoord thinks strong men make the world and the weak deserve to die – exactly the kind of vicious view that *Slaughterhouse-Five* seems to have been written to reject. But instead of telling us directly that Rumfoord is a douche, as he does with Roland Weary, the narrator lets Rumfoord's own thoughts incriminate him. After all, it's tough to sympathize with anyone who thinks the main character of the book you're reading is "a repulsive non-person."

Literary Devices

Symbols, Imagery, Allegory

The Horses

After the bombing of Dresden, Billy Pilgrim and several POWs return to the slaughterhouse to pick up souvenirs. Billy does not actually spend much time looking for things; he simply sits in a green, coffin-shaped horse-drawn wagon the POWs have been using and waits for his comrades. As Billy lies in his wagon in the afternoon sun, two German doctors approach him and scold him for the condition of his horses. The animals are desperately thirsty, and in their travel across the ashy rubble of Dresden, their hooves have cracked and broken so that every

step is agony. The horses are nearly mad with pain. Billy weeps for the first and last time during the war at the sight of these poor, abused animals (9.19-20).

Given that this scene is the only time Billy cries during the whole war, it must be pretty significant. In fact, the parallels between the horses' suffering and Billy's own seem striking. These horses have no way of understanding the destruction around them, nor the orders being given to them. With no way of protesting their treatment, they obediently keep walking through the ruins of Dresden even though every step on the sharp rocks damages their hooves. Like Billy himself, the animals are innocent victims of great suffering without ever understanding why. No wonder Billy finds himself in tears.

There is also a parallel between the horses and Roland Weary, the first character we see die in the book. Weary is the bully who attempts to shoot Billy before the Germans capture both of them. When the Germans take Weary prisoner, they force him to exchange his excellent boots for a pair of wooden clogs a German recruit is wearing. The clogs are so rough on Weary's feet that he injures himself marching, gets gangrene, and dies. Weary's bloodied feet appear at the beginning of Billy's wartime experience, and the horses' cracked hooves at the end. Perhaps the suffering of the horses reminds Billy of all of the terrible, pointless pain he has seen in this war, starting with foolish, violent Weary and ending with the Dresden firebombing.

The Stars

You may have noticed that the tiny sections in *Slaughterhouse-Five* are separated by little rows of three stars. These are not just there for decoration; Billy Pilgrim discovers that all Tralfamadorian books are laid out this way (5.3). The Tralfamadorians tell Billy that the stars contain their own short messages to create a single, beautiful scene.

Slaughterhouse-Five uses a lot of elements from the fictional part of the novel, and specifically from Billy's experiences on Tralfamadore, to structure the book as a whole. Not only do the stars in the Tralfamadorian novel appear throughout *Slaughterhouse-Five*, but the fact that the book is told out of chronological order fits the Tralfamadorian concept of time. (Check out Billy Pilgrim's "Character Analysis" for more on this). And the Tralfamadorian idea that there is no point in moralizing since we can't change the past or the future may explain why *Slaughterhouse-Five* does not offer a single, easy moral lesson.

By using elements from the made-up part of the novel to structure both the autobiographical *and* the fictional sections of *Slaughterhouse-Five*, Vonnegut suggests to the reader that all of Billy Pilgrim's adventures are part of the same overall narrative. The plot may distinguish between the narrator's and Billy's stories, but they both emerge from the same place: Vonnegut's efforts to write about the firebombing of Dresden. The structure of *Slaughterhouse-Five* never lets us forget that "Billy Pilgrim" is a thinly disguised fictional device Vonnegut can use to ponder the trauma of war – and the big questions of life and death – while still telling a pretty good story.

Prayer and Montana Wildhack's Locket
Montana Wildhack wears a locket on which is written, "God grant me the serenity to accept the things I cannot change, courage to change the things I can, and wisdom always to tell the difference" (9.33.21). The same words appear framed on Billy's optometry office wall in Chapter 3, Section 12. We find this prayer really striking for two reasons.

First, the prayer appears in both Billy's real life and his Tralfamadorian life, strongly hinting that his Tralfamadorian experiences are made up. He has taken bits and pieces from things he has seen in his daily life and read in science fiction novels to make up a world he wants to live in.

Second, this prayer expresses something profound that Billy is really looking for. He *does* want to find a way to accept what he cannot change (the past), the courage to change what he can (his current reality), and the wisdom to tell the difference. In a sense, Tralfamadore is all about granting this prayer: the Tralfamadorian belief in unchanging time means nothing *can* be changed, so there's Billy's serenity right there. And Billy's abduction gives him a perspective on his reality, which allows him to find the courage to tell the world about his new philosophy – to try to change humanity's sorrow and pain over death. It's pretty brave to try to change the world.

Note that even though this is a prayer, it's the Tralfamadorians that grant Billy this new serenity and courage, not God. God in the novel is strongly associated with the pain of death. Billy's mother's crucifix focuses on the agony of the crucifixion, and Kilgore Trout's two novels about Christ both emphasize his death and its purpose. Billy has seen enough pain and suffering among the innocent in his own life; he doesn't need Christianity to give him new examples. Instead of turning to the suffering Christ, Billy looks to space aliens for relief from his misery.

"Mustard Gas and Roses," "Nestled Like Spoons," and "Blue and Ivory"
A lot of the imagery in *Slaughterhouse-Five* repeats across sections and in different contexts. For example, the narrator describes his own breath when he is drunk as "mustard gas and roses" (1.3.2) – which is what his dog, Sandy, specifically does *not* smell like (1.4.14). This is also the odor of the corpses at Dresden a couple days after the firebombing, which Billy Pilgrim discovers as he digs through the rubble of the city in Chapter 10. This repetition of description serves to connect the "Billy Pilgrim" portion of the novel with the narrator's own personal memories and experiences.

Other examples of repetition of imagery include descriptions of characters "nestled like spoons": Billy and the hobo/private in the prison boxcar (3.29.3), Billy and his wife Valencia (4.1.2), and the American soldiers on the floor of the shed in the British compound (6.10.1) all nestle like spoons as they sleep.

There is also Billy's "ivory and blue" (4.1.4) bare feet as he walks barefoot through his Ilium, New York home, the "blue and ivory claw" (4.5.1) of his cold hand clinging to the vent in his boxcar on the way to a German POW center, and the "blue and ivory" (6.16.4) feet of the dead

hobo lying outside the train that will take Billy to Dresden.

The repetition of these phrases -- mustard gas and roses, nestled like spoons, and blue and ivory – demonstrates that no part of this story is isolated from any other. Each section, as brief as it may be, fits into a larger consideration of wartime and its aftermath. (By the way, for a discussion of the most famous repeated phrase in the whole book, "So it goes," check out our section on the theme of "Fate and Free Will.")

Setting

Germany, 1944-45; "Ilium," upstate New York

The setting of *Slaughterhouse-Five* is wide-ranging, but the two most important places are Germany during World War II and "Ilium," the fictional town in upstate New York where Billy Pilgrim lives most of his life.

In Germany Billy undergoes the painful experiences of captivity and violence that cause him to start skipping through time. And it's the narrator/author's real-life time in Dresden, Germany, that provokes him to write *Slaughterhouse-Five* in the first place. In Chapter 1, the narrator tells us that he and his wife spent some time after the war in Schenectady, New York, which Billy Pilgrim's "Ilium" seems to be based on. The parallels between the narrator and Billy's wartime and postwar experiences add to the sense that *Slaughterhouse-Five*, for all of its aliens and time travel, is a largely autobiographical novel.

Another recurring setting throughout the novel is the hospital. Billy spends his first night in the POW camp in the hospital, where he meets Edgar Derby doped up on morphine. When Billy has his breakdown and checks himself into a veteran's hospital after the war, he meets fellow veteran Eliot Rosewater and discovers the science-fiction novels that will help him escape from his awful life for the next 30 years. And when Billy is recovering from his plane crash in a hospital in Vermont in 1968, he first begins saying the name "Tralfamadore" aloud.

These three scenes of recovery strongly associate hospitals with relief. At the same time, these moments of rest from the stresses and memories that are driving him crazy are only temporary. Once Billy leaves the hospital, he always loses control again: his release from the prison hospital allows him to be shipped to Dresden; his departure from the veteran's hospital leads to his marriage with Valencia and the start of his dreary life as an optometrist; and his escape from the Vermont hospital sends him directly into conflict with his daughter, Barbara. While Vonnegut seems to represent the work that doctors do positively, medicine is still not *enough* to heal Billy of all that ails him. For that, the entire world would need to change.

Narrator Point of View

First Person (Peripheral Narrator)
The narrator is definitely a character in this novel: we get first-person sections in both the first and last chapters, and he pops up periodically throughout Billy's travels through Germany. The narrator also spends most of his time telling us about Billy rather than about his own life, which is why we can call him peripheral, on the sidelines.

At the same time, a lot of Billy's feelings and experiences seem to come from a third-person omniscient narrator, who has complete access to all of Billy's thoughts and feelings. This is not narration from the perspective of a person who is separate from the main character and making observations about his feelings. In some ways, Billy's story reads like a thinly veiled and fictionalized version of the narrator's own life. The lines between the perspectives of the narrator's "I" and Billy Pilgrim's "he" are actually pretty blurred.

Genre

Autobiography, Postmodern, Science Fiction, War Drama
Slaughterhouse-Five is not a pure autobiography because, while it does have elements of the author's life in it, most of the narrative is focused on a fictional character, Billy Pilgrim. At the same time, many of Vonnegut's own experiences in Dresden, Germany, provide the engine for *Slaughterhouse-Five*'s plot, so we think it deserves to be called a semi-autobiographical novel.

Slaughterhouse-Five is also primarily about various aspects of war: (a) how much it sucks, (b) how much it messes people up after it happens, and (c) how generally unfair life is that we have to go fight in wars and then grow old and die afterwards. So that's why we're also describing *Slaughterhouse-Five* as a war drama: not only does the plot focus on World War II, but the book also spends a lot of time pondering war as an experience.

As for the science fiction genre, *Slaughterhouse-Five* uses the elements of science fiction – time travel and aliens – but it is also self-conscious about considering what science fiction is *for*. Billy and Eliot Rosewater read science fiction because their own realities no longer make sense to them. They need invented realities that work by different rules because their own lives have lost meaning. *Slaughterhouse-Five* uses science fiction the same way it uses war, both as a plot point and as an object of philosophical examination.

The level of self-consciousness that *Slaughterhouse-Five* brings to the genres of autobiography, war drama, and science fiction all point to a fourth and final genre: the postmodern novel. The constant confusion about when – or even whether – the different events of the novel happen mean that readers are constantly kept at some distance from Billy Pilgrim and his life story. By

using the author as a character in the book and by telling Billy's story out of order, the novel itself keeps reminding us that Billy's story is fiction. This manner of storytelling indicates a degree of skepticism about the idea of a unified self or the possibility of realistic narration that characterizes postmodernism.

Tone

Spare, Elusive, Deadpan

As you'll know the second you look at a page of *Slaughterhouse-Five*, the book is broken into tiny, tiny sections. Most of these sections are pretty action-packed, so the narrator doesn't leave himself much space to wax lyrical about the events he is relating. The narration in the book is stripped bare of much description, so it's hard to tell what kind of emotional message the narrator is trying to get across.

In fact, the narrator seems kind of grossed out by big displays of emotion. He likes the fact that Billy doesn't cry out loud, and even gives silent crying its own epigraph (see "What's Up With the Epigraph?"). He also describes emotion in pretty unsympathetic terms. When Valencia hears that her husband has been in a plane crash, the narrator says:

Valencia adored Billy. She was crying and yelping so hard as she drove that she missed the correct turnoff from the throughway. (9.1.3)

This is kind of cruel for a number of reasons: (1) we know Billy doesn't feel as much for Valencia as she does for him; and (2), "yelping" is a pretty insulting way to describe a woman sobbing over her husband's potentially fatal injury. The narrator really doesn't appear to think much of emotion, and his descriptions of events reflect this distaste.

Yet, at the same time, the narrator is telling us about the horrors of war. He is describing horrific events that have huge meaning for him personally. Even if he doesn't tell us directly how to feel about these events, he does convey a lot of pathos by appealing to the audience's emotions. We call the tone of *Slaughterhouse-Five* elusive because there is a lot of emotion in this book, but it's hard to pin down. The narrator rarely says outright: this sucks. But he *shows* that it does. For example, in the aftermath of the Dresden firebombing, when Billy, the other POWs, and their German guards crawl through the rubble, the narrator tells us:

American fighter planes came in under the smoke to see if anything was moving. They saw Billy and the rest moving down there. The planes sprayed them with machine-gun bullets, but the bullets missed. Then they saw some other people moving down by the riverside and they shot at them. They hit some of them. So it goes.

The idea was to hasten the end of the war. (8.27.1-2)

There are no adjectives in this passage, nothing like "tragic" or "terrifying," to describe what it would be like for an American POW to be shot at by American fighter pilots trying to kill everything they see. Yet, at the same time, *because* there is so little emotional description, the overall impact of the scene seems much bigger than you would expect from such a brief passage. The fact that Billy escapes with his life just by random chance, because the bullets miss – and that the "other people moving down by the riverside" aren't so lucky, also by random chance – emphasizes how meaningless life and death seem in this devastated wartime landscape.

The final sentence, that "The idea was to hasten the end of the war," really clinches the deadpan emotional effect of this scene. These pilots may have been deployed to put a decisive end to German resistance, but in reality, on the ground, who are the fighter planes shooting at? *American POWs*. In just a few words, the narrator manages to convey rage, frustration, and sorrow over the confusion and destructiveness of wartime. This book really does get us every time.

Writing Style

Dry, Stark

As we discuss in our "Tone" section, there aren't too many adjectives floating around *Slaughterhouse-Five*. The novel's writing is minimalist and dry, and Vonnegut tends to write in short, declarative sentences. Each tiny section is dense with dialogue and action. For example, check out Chapter 3, Section 29 (and bear in mind, this is the *whole* section):

The war was nearly over. The locomotives began to move east in late December. The war would end in May. German prisons everywhere were absolutely full, and there was no longer any food for the prisoners to eat, and no longer any fuel to keep them warm. And yet – here came more prisoners. (3.29.1)

This brief passage tells us (a) when the events of this part of the book are taking place (late December) and (b) what waits in the immediate future (the end of the war). It also outlines the main problems that Billy Pilgrim faces as a POW during this part of the war: (a) there is no room for him in German prisons, (b) there is no food for him to eat, and (c) there is nothing to keep him warm.

Still, even amidst all this straightforward, unadorned writing, there is an element of black humor. The book sets out the terrible conditions Billy will be living with, but it doesn't stop there. It adds the awful irony that, even though these conditions are so terrible, the war keeps making them worse by piling on more and more prisoners. *Slaughterhouse-Five* is filled with blunt, grim ironies like this one, which is why we describe its style as stark.

What's Up With the Title?

Though you know this book as *Slaughterhouse-Five*, the full title is actually *Slaughterhouse-Five, or the Children's Crusade: A Duty-Dance With Death* . When main character Billy Pilgrim winds up in Dresden, Germany, as a prisoner of war (POW) in World War II, he and a hundred other American POWs are kept in an abandoned slaughterhouse called Slaughterhouse-Five. That is the strict plot-level meaning of the title. But we can't ignore the larger metaphor of the title: after all, this is an anti-war book, and what is war except slaughter?

There is also a third level of meaning to the title, which is biographical. Obviously, this book is fiction: there's plenty of aliens and time travel to go around. But there's also a ton of biographical detail from Kurt Vonnegut's own life in these pages, including the fact that he was (yes, you guessed it) an American POW in the city of Dresden during the infamous Dresden firebombing.

Vonnegut survived the bombing by sheltering in an underground meat locker on the grounds of the slaughterhouse where he was a prisoner (source: Klinkowitz, Jerome. *Slaughterhouse-Five: Reforming the Novel and the World*. Boston: Twayne Publishers, 1990. Pg. 3). So Slaughterhouse-Five is: (a) where Billy Pilgrim, the main character, winds up during the war; (b) figuratively, what war *is*; and (c) where Kurt Vonnegut, author, actually spent several months at the end of World War II.

Then there is a second part to the title, *The Children's Crusade* . The Children's Crusade was a real historical event and also a giant wartime screw-up. Fired up by the religious fanaticism of the day (by which we mean thirteenth-century medieval Europe), a boy named Nicholas Cologne inspired thousands of children and teens to marched out of France and Germany to go Jerusalem to join the Crusades. It's unclear if any of these kids ever made it to Jerusalem; many turned back and it's likely that most of them died along the journey (source). So the Children's Crusade, a pointless sacrifice of innocent life, relates to the novel's anti-war themes.

The Children's Crusade has heavy symbolic weight in this particular book. The narrator (a Vonnegut stand-in) says that he promised the wife of his war buddy that he would call his war book *The Children's Crusade* so that it would never be misinterpreted as a *heroic* war story (1.11). *Slaughterhouse-Five* may be about war, but it sure as hell ain't about heroes. It's a book about innocents sent to fight a war they do not understand, who suffer terrible things for no reason. This sounds a lot like a Children's Crusade to us.

Last but not least, how about that *Duty-Dance With Death*? The narrator is quoting the French writer Céline here, who said that all art depends on a dance with death. Céline, who fought for France in World War I, claims that he has spent his entire life "waltz[ing death] around" (1.20.2). Billy Pilgrim also spends most of his life engaging with death – seeing it in his dreams, traveling

back to it in time, trying to avoid it with the Tralfamadorians. But neither Billy's nor the narrator's dance with death is voluntary. Both of them have fought in a war beyond their control and not of their choosing. So this is not a willing dance with death; it's a duty-dance with death.

What's Up With the Epigraph?

"The cattle are lowing,
The Baby awakes.
But the little Lord Jesus
No crying He makes"These four lines appear in one of the most famous Christmas carols ever, "Away in a Manger." (Listen to it here!) Although we could speculate endlessly about why Vonnegut picks this particular Christmas carol for his epigraph, the author makes the reader's job a little easier by giving us a reason. In Chapter 9, Section 20, the narrator comments that main character Billy Pilgrim always cries silently when he weeps after the war. He weeps very little, even though he has "seen a lot of things to cry *about*" (9.21.2). In other words, like the baby Jesus, "no crying he makes." For more on Billy's character, check out his "Character Analysis."

Vonnegut does this kind of thing all the time in *Slaughterhouse-Five*: making a reference to a Christmas carol or a novel or a history book. And he'll also include the reasons *why* he does so. He just doesn't always include the explanation next to the reference itself.

Slaughterhouse-Five is like a wordy version of a scavenger hunt, where you have to search through the whole book to find the clues you're looking for. The epigraph appears just before the first page of the book, but we only get direct comments on what it means in the second-to-last chapter. For more on the circular structure of the book, check out "What's Up With the Ending?"

What's Up With the Ending?

One of Billy Pilgrim's big obsessions is this unchanging idea of time that he claims to get from the toilet plunger-shaped aliens of the planet of Tralfamadore. (Seriously.) According to the Tralfamadorians, each single moment in time goes on forever. It is an Earthling illusion to think of time moving forward or backward, because all of these moments take place at once, simultaneously.

This matters because Billy's ideas also influence the shape of the novel itself. The weird thing about the ending of *Slaughterhouse-Five* is that it actually comes in the beginning and the middle of the novel as much as it does at the end. In the final section of the book, we get scenes of: (a) the aftermath of the Dresden firebombing (see "In a Nutshell" for more on this); (b) the execution of high school teacher and American POW Edgar Derby for stealing a teapot from the ruins of the city; and (c) a bird tweeting at Billy Pilgrim.

All of that stuff, though – the firebombing of Dresden, Edgar Derby, even the bird – also comes into the first chapter of the novel. In the beginning of *Slaughterhouse-Five*, the narrator tells us that this novel is about Dresden, he discusses poor old Edgar Derby with his war buddy, Bernard O'Hare – hell, he even informs us that the novel "ends like this: *Poo-tee-weet*?" (1.22.12).

In other words, throughout the book, references to future and past events intermingle. For example, we know that poor old Edgar Derby, even while he's walking around in Billy's memories, has already been shot. At the same time that Billy listens to a barbershop quartet at his wedding anniversary party in Chapter 8, he remembers his German guards seeing the destruction of Dresden in 1945 (8.22.1). There is a real sense that everything happens simultaneously in this book, and we just get to some things before others thanks to the order of the pages.

One last word on the last word of the book: right in the first chapter, the narrator tells us that birds say "[a]ll there is to say about a massacre, things like *Poo-tee-weet*?" (1.15.2). And the final phrase of *Slaughterhouse-Five*, following a depiction of the massacre at Dresden, is, of course: *Poo-tee-weet?* This book is like one of those nested Russian dolls where you open one and inside is a smaller version of the exact same thing: nearly every chapter foreshadows what's coming next and looks back at what has just come before it. So it's hard to say where the stories of Billy Pilgrim and the narrator truly begin and end, except that there is a first page and a last page to the book.

Did You Know?

Trivia

- In addition to his work in anthropology at the University of Chicago, Vonnegut also studied chemistry pretty extensively (source). In fact, he also felt very strongly that, "Literature should not disappear up its own asshole, so to speak" (source). In other words, we should be encouraging scientists and doctors to write more – fiction should not just be the work of explicitly literary people. So take note, future chemists, biologists, and doctors of the world! Consider following in Vonnegut's footsteps and writing fiction.
- Unlike Billy Pilgrim, Vonnegut was *not* drafted into the military in World War II. He joined up voluntarily in 1942 and was given supplemental engineering training before heading out to Luxembourg to fight the Battle of the Bulge. (source)
- Vonnegut struggled all his life with depression, culminating in a suicide attempt in 1984. He survived this attempt and passed away over twenty years later, at the age of 84, on April 12, 2007. (source)

Steaminess Rating

R

The sex in *Slaughterhouse-Five* isn't very *sexy*. We know that people are having it, but it is never described very intensely. Still, there is a fair amount. Billy Pilgrim cheats on his wife in the laundry room of a friend's house during a party in Chapter 2, Section 29. We get a pretty clinical description of Billy impregnating Valencia in Chapter 5, Section 46. And Billy dreams about porn star Montana Wildhack (his partner in the Tralfamadorian zoo) in Chapter 5, Section 65. Billy also visits a pornographic bookstore in Chapter 9, among other scattered references to sex. So there is plenty of sex in *Slaughterhouse-Five*, but it's not a central theme.

Allusions and Cultural References

Literary and Philosophical References

- "*Eheu, fugaces laburuntur anni,*" Latin quote from Horace: "*Alas, our fleeting years pass away*" (1.9.1)
- *Extraordinary Popular Delusions and the Madness of Crowds*, Charles Mackay (1.12.1)
- *Dresden, History, Stage and Gallery*, Mary Endell (1.12.10)
- Johann Wolfgang von Goethe (1.12.14)
- *Words for the Wind*, Theodore Roethke (1.20.1)
- *Céline and His Vision*, Erika Ostrovsky (1.20.1-3)
- *Death on the Installment Plan*, Louis Ferdinand Céline (1.20.3)
- The Gideon Bible (1.21.1-5)
- Martin Luther (2.12.1)
- *The Execution of Private Slovik*, William Bradford Huie (2.27.2)
- *Valley of the Dolls*, Jacqueline Susann (5.2.1)
- *Red Badge of Courage*, Stephen Crane (5.18.2)
- *The Brother's Karamazov* , Fyodor Dostoevsky (5.21.1)
- *The New Testament* (5.30.5)
- Scheherazade, from *One Thousand and One Arabian Nights* (5.49.1)
- Kin Hubbard, playwright (5.56.2)
- The land of Oz from *The Wonderful Wizard of Oz* (6.17.3)
- *Ivanhoe*, Sir Walter Scott (8.11.3)
- *The Destruction of Dresden*, David Irving (9.5.1)
- George Jean Nathan, critic (9.24.1)
- Norman Mailer, author and playwright (9.33.1)
- *Uncle Tom's Cabin* , Harriet Beecher Stowe (9.33.1)

- *The Three Musketeers* (2.24.3, 2.31.10, 2.32.2)

Historical References

- The firebombing of Dresden
- The atomic bombing of Hiroshima (1.6.3, 9.4.4, 9.4.8-13)
- Nazi concentration camps (1.6.3)
- The Children's Crusade (1.11.2, 5.27.9)
- George Washington (1.13.1)
- The Civil War (2.27.2)
- Earl Warren (3.5.2)
- Sir Isaac Newton and the Third Law of Motion (4.12.1)
- Battle of Dunkirk (5.27.1)
- Queen Elizabeth I of England (5.45.10)
- Christopher Columbus (5.45.10)
- Green Berets, Vietnam (3.14.1, 5.45.9, 5.46.1, 5.51.9, 9.8.2)
- President John F. Kennedy (5.49.2)
- Napoleonic times (1803-1815) (5.57.2)
- Hill 875 near Dakto, Vietnam (5.65.2)
- Ronald Reagan (9.1.3)
- Ira C. Eaker, Lieutenant General, U.S.A.F. (9.5.1)
- British Air Marshal Sir Robert Saundby (9.5.1)
- Charles Darwin, British naturalist (10.2.1)

Cultural and Pop Culture References

- "My name is Yon Yonson" children's song (1.2.4)
- Harrison Starr, director (1.2.7-12)
- *Mutt and Jeff*, comic strip (1.3.16)
- New York World's Fair (1.9.1, 1.13.1)
- John Wayne (1.10.18)
- Frank Sinatra (1.10.18)
- Walt Disney (1.13.1)
- "A Mighty Fortress Is Our God," hymn (2.12.1)
- Johann Sebastian Bach (2.12.1)
- The Iron Maiden of Nuremberg (2.17.4)
- Louis Daguerre (2.23.2)
- André Le Fèvre (2.23.2-4)
- The "Mona Lisa," painted by Leonardo da Vinci (3.8.1)

- "Hail, Hail, the Gang's All Here," *Pirates of Penzance*, Gilbert and Sullivan (5.11.7)
- Cinderella (5.15.2, 5.53.4, 5.55.2, 6.11)
- "The Spirit of '76 ," American painting by Archibald MacNeal Willard (6.9.1)
- "Wait Till the Sun Shines, Nelly," popular song (7.4.1)
- "That Old Gang of Mine," popular song (8.14.1)
- "'Leven Cent Cotton, Forty Cent Meat," popular song (8.19.2)

Best of the Web

Film and Theater Productions

Slaughterhouse-Five, 1972
http://www.imdb.com/title/tt0069280/
This film version stars a bunch of people we've never heard of.

Slaughterhouse-Five, the Opera
http://www.vonnegutweb.com/sh5/sh5_opera.html
Seriously. Our link is to the 1996 review by Anne Midgette in *Munich Found*.

Slaughterhouse-Five, the Play
http://www.vonnegutweb.com/sh5/sh5_steppenwolf.html
1996 review Associated Press review by Michael Kuchwara.

Videos

Jon Stewart Interviews Vonnegut
http://www.thedailyshow.com/watch/tue-september-13-2005/kurt-vonnegut
When Vonnegut died two years after this 2005 interview, Jon Stewart paid tribute to him at the end of an episode by putting up a screen that read, "So it goes."

PBS Interview with Kurt Vonnegut
http://www.youtube.com/watch?v=tdANElmRU6k
A tribute to Vonnegut that aired after his death in 2007.

A Subtitled Serbian Production of the Play
http://www.youtube.com/watch?v=IKYN-8TLiKU&feature=PlayList&p=7CA18893F97DD546&playnext=1&playnext_from=PL&index=51
The steady-cam makes us a little seasick. Also, why so *serious*?

"Visiting Slaughterhouse-Five in Germany"

http://www.youtube.com/watch?v=wwmmApAUQG0
This guy goes to the original slaughterhouse where Vonnegut was a prisoner of war.

Images

Kurt Vonnegut as a Young Man
http://www.oneparticularwave.com/wp-content/uploads/vonnegut.jpg
Well, here he is.

Photograph of Kurt Vonnegut as an Older Man
http://www.shsu.edu/~eng_wpf/authors/pictures/vonnegut.jpg
Well, here he is again.

Kurt Vonnegut: Gallery of Photographs
http://www.kurt-vonnegut.com/photo.shtml
This is a really comprehensive series of photographs of Vonnegut from babyhood to old age. A life told in pictures!

Websites

"15 Things Kurt Vonnegut Said Better Than Anyone Else Ever Has or Will"
http://www.avclub.com/articles/15-things-kurt-vonnegut-said-better-than-anyone-el,1858/
The Onion A.V. Club does good work: these excerpts from Vonnegut's novels really give us a broad sense of his work as a whole. Of course, this list includes one of the most famous three-word quotes of all time, taken from *Slaughterhouse-Five*: "So it goes."

Vonnegut's Official Biography
http://www.vonnegut.com/artist.asp
This biography provides some details about Vonnegut's life and also focuses on his development as a visual artist. Two of his own illustrations make it into *Slaughterhouse-Five*: Billy Pilgrim's dream tombstone and Montana Wildhack's breasts with her locket hanging between them.

Original *New York Times* Review of *Slaughterhouse-Five*
http://www.vonnegutweb.com/sh5/sh5_nytimes.html
They liked it.

The Banning of *Slaughterhouse-Five*
http://solonor.com/bannedbooks/archives/001789.html
As you might expect, with all its sex, violence, and religious skepticism, *Slaughterhouse-Five* has often been banned, including in many school libraries.

"How to Write With Style"
http://www.google.com/url?sa=t&source=web&ct=res&cd=1&ved=0CAcQFjAA&url=http%3A%2F%2Fpublic.lanl.gov%2Fkmh%2Fpc-24-66-vonnegut.pdf&ei=wtNwS4XhAYKMtAOG4ribCA&us

g=AFQjCNEyu9U4SPqCdb2irT8qldh7KzPBng&sig2=_dTWRWao-bkj0KqjN-ItGQ
Kurt Vonnegut tells us directly how to write with style. We know we're taking notes on this one. [PDF file]

Printed in Great Britain
by Amazon.co.uk, Ltd.,
Marston Gate.